FLOYD CLYMER'S

Historical

MOTOR SCRAPBOOK

FOREIGN CAR EDITION

VOLUME 1

Many of the early 4-wheel vehicles had unique methods of propulsion, such as this one horsepower (no pun) which was used in England in 1829.

Published by

FLOYD CLYMER

World's Largest Publisher of Books Relating to Automobiles, Motorcycles, Motor Racing, and Americana

1268 SO. ALVARADO STREET   LOS ANGELES 6, CALIFORNIA

STYLISH PROMENADERS ON THE PARIS BOULEVARDS
IN 1900 DRIVING A 5CV DECAUVILLE

INDEX — FOREIGN CAR SCRAPBOOK — VOL. 1

A

Adams 100
A. F. N. 190
Airex 81
Alberghi Electric Omnibus 95
Allard Special 208
Allday's Traveler Voiturette 29, 82
Anglian Light Car 64
Argyll 83, 99
Ariel 101
Armstrong-Siddeley 156, 172
Arrol-Johnston Engine 70
Aston-Martin 198
A-T Speedometer 116
Austin 109, 125, 150, 169
Auto Union 206
Avon 187

B

Bayliss-Thomas 129
Beatonson Patent One-Man Hood 123
Belle Car 37
Belsize 122
Benz Powered Tricycle, 1885 20
Benz, 1898 26
Bira, B. 179
B.K. Motor Accessories 59
B.M.W. 203
Bosch 179
Bowden Accessories 137
Bowden Handlebar Control System 43
Brauchitsch 179
British Salmson 183
Brooke 102
Brough Superior 188, 204
Brown Gear Driven Car 57
B.S.A. with Fluid Drive 155, 160, 177
B.S.A. Scout 210

C

Canterbury 42
Car Pup Trailer 191
Caracciola, Rudolf 179, 222
Carpeviam Car 39
Chevrolet of Canada 205
Church Steam Vehicle, 1832 20
Citroen 148, 159, 215
Classic Calcott 127
Clement 86
Cluley 130
Clyde 60
Clymer, Floyd 3
Crestmobile Front Wheel Drive 45
Crossley Saloon with self-changing gears.. 157
Cubitt 131
Cupelle 66
Cyclone Motor 34, 35
Cynophere Dog-powered Vehicle 22

D

Daimler's First Vehicle, 1855 21
Daimler 140, 212
Daimler, with Fluid Drive 153, 154
Darracq 50, 87
De Dion Bouton 106
Deasy 104
Delahaye 181
Dinin Accumulators 80
DKW 206
Dorman Engine 114
Ducellier Lamps 80
Duco Motor Accessories 47
Dudgon's Steam Vehicle, 1868 21

E

Early Auto Clothing 76
Enfield 87
Englebert Tyres 202

E (con't)

Evans "Orukter Amphibolos," 1805 20
Eyston, George E. T. 163

F

Fafnir Car & Engine 69, 118
Fagioli 179
Fairfield, P. G. 179
Fiat 94, 108, 173, 216
Fitzmaurice 194
Florentia 96
Flying Standard 221
F. N. 117
Ford Prefect 218, 219
Ford Saloon 193
Frazer-Nash 203
Friswell-Standard 79
Front Wheel Drive Vehicle powered
by Dog, 1870 26

G

Gamage Car & Accessories 49, 72
Gilburt Light Car 61
Gladiator 74, 104
Glasgow Farm Tractor 126
Gordon Miniature 48
Gordon Steam Carriage of 1829 24
Gregoire 91

H

Hammonia Vehicles of Germany 36
Hancock's Steam Vehicle of 1836 19
Hansa 199
Higate Cars 41, 58
Hillman 135, 145, 182
Horbick Minor 55
Howes, Bobby 189
Humber 54, 63, 149, 213

I

Indian 110
Iris 78
Isotta Fraschini 98

J

Jacksons 75
James & Browne Light Car 65
James Steam Coach of 1829 24
Jensen 207
Jensen Coachwork (Ford Chassis) 174
Jones Speedometer 123
Jowett 152, 197

K

Kempshall Tyres 121

L

Lagonda 171
Lammas-Graham 189
Lanchester with Epicyclic Change
Speed Gear 132
Lanchester with Fluid Drive 153
Lanchester Road Rider 209
Leonard "Avant-Train" 41
Lookers Ltd., Specialists in Automobiles .. 115

M

Marchand 95
Marcus Australian Vehicle of 1873 23
Marcus, Siegfried—Vehicle of 1875 19
Maudslay 112
Mays, Raymond 179
Mercedes-Benz 168, 211, 222
MG 161, 178, 224
Michelin Tyres 97, 113
Minerva 84
Missing Link Vehicle...28, 29, 30, 31, 32, 33
Mobile 46

M (con't)

Mobiloil	220
Morgan Motor Bodies	83
Morgan 4	200
Morris	167
Morris-Oxford	111, 151
Motor Car Houses	128

N

Napier	103, 124
N.S.U. Vetturette	110

O

O.H.B. Light Touring Car	43
Olympia Show of 1923	138, 139
Opel	186, 201

P

1923 Paris Salon (Auto Show)	141, 142, 143, 144
Paul, Cyril	179
Pennington Autocar of 1896	25
Perry's Fore-Carriage	38
Phoenix Quadcar	68
Phoenix Trimo	53
Porthos	93

Q

Quadrant Tri-Car	52

R

Railton	164
Rapier	180
Reader	62
Renault	147, 165, 185
Reo with British Coachwork	92
Riley	166
Riley Tri-Car	67
Riley Two-Seater	88
Rolls-Royce	73, 146
Rosemeyer, Berndt	179
Rover	134, 162, 192

R (con't)

Rover Laundalettes & Station Cabs	105
Runabaken Spark Tester & Amplifier	128

S

Saunders Petrol Saver	115
Seaman, Richard	179
Silent Bell Car	77
Simms	56
Singer Forecar	51
Solex	196
Spykers	87
SS	163
Standard	158, 170
Star	37, 90
Starling	89
Steam Power Vehicle	23
Stirling Dogcart	42
Stuck	179
Sunbeam	120, 175
Sunbeam-Talbot	214
Swift Brougham	71

T

Talbot	85, 107
Tarrant's First Australian Car	27
Thompson's Steam Car	27
Tickford	176
Trevithich Steam Road Carriage of 1802	24
Triumph-Dolomite	217

V

Vauxhall	44, 176, 184
Vortex Silencer	191
Vulcan	119, 136

W

Waddington Voiturette	39
West-Astor Doctor's Laundalette	91
White & Poppe Engines	66
Wolf Motette	40
Wolseley	133, 195

My Scrapbook of Foreign Cars

By FLOYD CLYMER

My father, Dr. J. B. Clymer, a general practitioner so common in small towns before the days of the specialists, purchased the first automobile to be sold north of Denver in the State of Colorado. We lived in the little town of Berthoud, situated in a fertile farming valley nine miles east of the foothills of the Colorado Rocky Mountains.

The car was a single-cylinder curved dash Oldsmobile with tiller steering. It created a sensation in our community, and I think Dad lost a few patients who had no confidence in his ability to get to their homes while driving that noisy smelly contraption then known as the horseless carriage. I can recall as a youngster of seven, while riding with Dad, our car causing a few runaways and the natives standing on the sidewalks and alongside the country roads with an awed look as we passed by at a speed of at least 15 miles per hour. Many were skeptical that the automobile would ever be a success.

By 1905, we had graduated to a big 7 H.P. single-cylinder Reo principally because Dad wanted a car with wheel steering and more power. So one can see that there was a "horsepower race" on even in the early days. By the time I was eleven, I was a full-fledged automobile dealer handling Reo, Maxwell, and Cadillac cars. In those days, no dealer licenses or showrooms were required. There were so many makes offered the public that almost anyone who would buy a car could secure the agency in a small community providing the dealership was open. By selling a Reo to my Dad, a Maxwell to a local merchant, Ed McCormick, and a Cadillac to a Johnstown business man, Cy Waite, I secured the agencies for these three popular makes. In two years, I had sold twenty-six cars and when four-cylinder cars became more popular, I became a dealer for Studebaker—EMF "30" and Flanders "20", and did a fair business with these cars.

Very often I made trips to Denver, the capital city of Colorado, some fifty miles from Berthoud. Here I always visited the showrooms which were even then very numerous and located along Broadway, the automobile row of the city. Of course, I attended the annual automobile shows held in Denver's early Coliseum and later in the Mammoth Skating Rink and City Auditorium.

Occasionally, a foreign car passed through Berthoud, but seldom did I have a chance to inspect one carefully. And, of course, the Denver shows afforded this opportunity because there were several foreign cars always exhibited each year.

Having never owned a foreign car in my early days as a dealer, I was always intrigued with some of the features that were unlike our American cars. I well remember the small De de Dion, and the dealer in Denver was kind enough to let me drive one a few miles. This little car with a single-cylinder vertical engine mounted under the hood and built in France was a quality car in its day.

Another French car that seemed fantastic to me at that time was the large Renault. The long sloping hood of this car looked somewhat like our own air-cooled Franklins of the twenties. The radiator was back of the hood directly in front of the cowl, and it had a powerful and, for its day, a dependable engine.

Judge E. A. Colburn, who was also an expert sulky racehorse driver, was the dealer. He operated the Colburn Automobile Co., and later on decided to build a car bearing the Colburn name which he did. Many of the features of the first Colburns, including the sloping hood, were copied from Renault design by Mr. Colburn.

But the car that intrigued me the most was the very high-priced British Rolls-Royce. There were a few of these cars in Denver, and owned only by the wealthy people because of the car's high price. A few small foreign three-wheelers were also to be seen on the streets of Denver. I remember one small French car, the Richard, did quite well in local sales. The French Panhard was another one of the popular foreign cars.

Foreign built tires were quite popular especially the British Dunlop and the French Michelin. Both of these tires were sold by distributors in Denver.

Some of the foreign cars had what I thought were very funny headlights, and several had automatic inlet valves instead of mechanical. They opened by the suction of the piston on its down stroke instead of by a cam and a push rod.

Being a reader of all of the motor magazines, I had heard of the other makes of foreign cars that were being sold in the large cities such as New York and Chicago, but some of them I had never seen. I made a practice of writing for and usually receiving a catalog on every make of foreign automobile manufactured as well as U.S. built cars in those early days. Most of these I have kept throughout the years, and with my large library of books, photographs, magazines, and other information on American cars, I have been able to compile about 150 books dealing with almost every phase of the automobile industry.

In compiling this Scrapbook of Foreign Automobiles, I want to make it clear that no effort has been made to compile a complete list, and of course, only a very small percentage of foreign makes are illustrated or described in this book. It would take a thousand volumes of this size book to cover all of the various makes and models that were manufactured by our pioneering friends across the sea.

While much of the information in this book is compiled from my library of early day catalogs, many of the advertisements came from early publications. While many of these magazines are no longer published, many of them are, and listed below are magazines from which some of the material that appears in this book was secured.

They are as follows: Motor World, King's Highway, Century Magazine, Country Life, Autocar, Vanity Fair, Cycle Car, Illustrated Sporting & Dramatic News, Motor Sport, Light Car, Rivista Mensile, U.S. National Museum Folder, Das Auto, Speed, L'Illustration, History of Motorized Vehicles, London Transport, Illustrated London News, and the Literary Digest.

In publishing this book I feel that we are doing something to preserve for future historians and collectors the records of many long-forgotten, but one time famous makes of early foreign cars. I trust this book will be of interest to all automotive enthusiasts.

Floyd Clymer

SOME EARLY PROJECTS

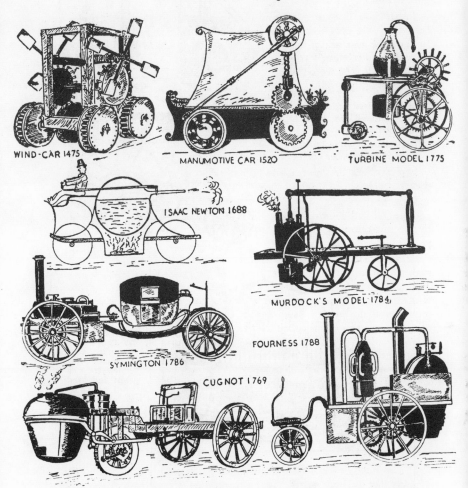

WIND-CAR 1475

MANUMOTIVE CAR 1520

TURBINE MODEL 1775

ISAAC NEWTON 1688

MURDOCK'S MODEL 1784

FOURNESS 1788

SYMINGTON 1786

CUGNOT 1769

There were a number of vehicles built to travel over land impelled by sails, but the one shown above (top left) being moved by rotation of the wheels may be considered a motor car. The manumotive car belonged to the Emperor Maximilian, and is from a drawing by A. Dürer. A man walked on each side working the long 'piston-poles,' and it is said that more men were inside working cranks. The turbine model was a watchmaker's toy; the steam-jet thrusting on the vanes of the rotor caused the wheels to turn. Newton's jet-propelled car never got beyond the projection; Murdock and Symington built working models, and these, together with the Cugnot and Fourness cars, which actually ran.

Trevithick was one of the greatest steam engine inventors, and he progressed from a small model on three wheels to really practical road carriages. Most of his time, however, was given to railway work.

The sources from which these drawings are taken may be apocryphal

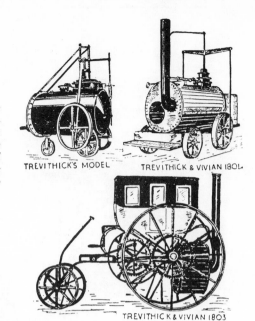

TREVITHICK'S MODEL

TREVITHICK & VIVIAN 1801.

TREVITHICK & VIVIAN 1803

LEFT — In 1824 this unique vehicle was propelled by two horses using the treadmill principle. It was built and used in London, England, by W. F. Snowden.

LEFT — In 1833 this Church Steam Coach was built and operated in England.

8

Griffiths' road coach,
built 1821

JAMES 1824

JAMES 1830

BURSTALL & HILL 1824

BURSTALL & HILL 1825

FRASER 1830

GORDON 1828

GURNEY 1829

GURNEY 1827

Walter Hancock, probably the best-known of early road-car builders, was unlucky in his business dealings and had to abandon his projects

IN 1834 THIS HANCOCK SAIL WAGON
APPEARED ON THE ROADS NEAR LONDON, ENGLAND.

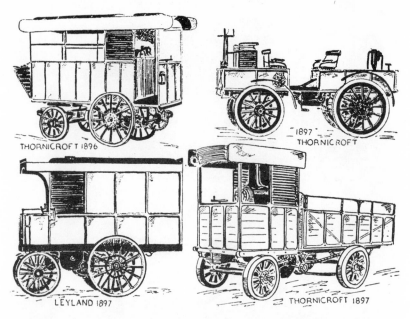

*The first English vehicles of the new steam era: the fore-runners of the
steam lorries and buses which became so numerous before the Great War*

*Mr. Ricketts driving his steam car, 1859
(From a contemporary sketch in ' The Illustrated London News ')*

One of the first Benz cars, built in 1885. From the original in the Science Museum, London

A well-known type of one-cylindered motor tricycle, the Leon Bollée, which came out in 1896

The original Lanchester Phaeton, 1896

Britain's First Car..

To Lanchester belongs the honour of being the very first British 4-wheeled petrol-driven car. To Lanchester, since that historic day over fifty years ago, also belong many subsequent 'firsts.' Lanchester engineering has in fact been an inspiration to the whole motoring industry.

Compagnie des Automobiles et Moteurs Henriod

7-9 Rue de Sablonville, Neuilly
(Porte-Maillot) :: France

Carriages with 5 to 12 horse-power motors with flange-cooled cylinders.

Three-seat carriages with 4 horse power motors with flange-cooled cylinders.

1899

The only carriage with an 8 horse-power motor not cooled by a water-jacket, which took part in the Paris-Bordeaux race, was a Henriod Carriage that made 321 miles in 19 hours.

These motors are vapor, petroleum, and alcohol engines.

Carburation is effected by means of a vaporizer.

INTERNATIONAL

: DOCTOR'S CAR :

1899

Supplied with or without Hood, which is detachable

MORE doctors are users of this car than all other patterns put together. It is extremely reliable, very comfortable, and economical in use. It is a handsome carriage, and a credit to its owner and user. It will mount the steepest hills with ease, and can travel at a great speed on the level. It will carry enough oil for two hundred miles, and cannot catch on fire or explode. Over 1,600 of these motors are in use on the Continent and in England.

International Motor Car Co.

15, High Road, Kilburn, London, W.

Société des Anciens Etablissements
PANHARD & LEVASSOR

19 Avenue d'Ivry   PARIS, FRANCE

CAPITALIZED AT 5,000,000 FRANCS

MR. RENÉ DE KNYFF'S AUTOMOBILE—12 H.-P.

HORSELESS CARRIAGES

with 2, 4, 6, 8 seats and more, driven by

PETROLEUM MOTORS

of 4, 6, 8, 10, 12, 16 and 20 Horse-Power.

1899

PHAETONS	COUPÉS	VIS–À–VIS
CARTS	LANDAUS	COMMERCIAL
WAGONETTES	LANDAULETS	TRAVELERS'
FAMILY OMNIBUSES	CABS	CARRIAGES
TRAVELING CARRIAGES	VICTORIAS	DELIVERY WAGONS

Omnibuses and Large Breaks, with a seating
capacity of 20, for public passenger service

Trucks for Heavy Traffic

(Maximum Capacity 2¾ Tons)

High-Speed Automobiles for Railways
Tramways
Decauville Traction-Engines

PETROLEUM LAUNCHES

16

Les Souverains Européens caricaturés en 1899

1. S. M. l'Empereur de Russie. — 2. S. M. Léopold II, Roi des Belges. — 3. S. M. Victoria, Reine d'Angleterre. — 4. S. M. la Reine Wilhelmine de Hollande. — 5. S. A. R. le Prince de Galles. — 6. M. Félix Faure, Président de la République Française. — 7. S. M. Charles 1er, Roi de Portugal. — 8. S. M. Guillaume II, Empereur d'Allemagne. — 9. S. M. François-Joseph II, Empereur d'Autriche. — 10. S. M. Alphonse XIII, Roi d'Espagne. — 11. S. M. Humbert 1er, Roi d'Italie.

A 1912 Thornycroft charabanc

**A small steam omnibus which ran in London
in the late 'nineties**

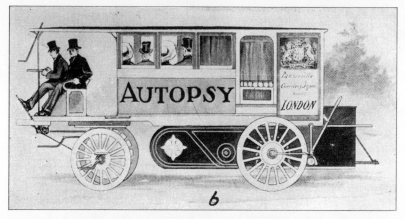

a, Cugnot's vehicle of 1770, now preserved in the Conservatoire National des Arts et Métiers at Paris. Photograph No. 38679.

b, One of Walter Hancock's steam vehicles, 1836. Photograph No. 31710–F.

c, Gasoline-powered vehicle of Siegfried Marcus, 1875. Photograph No. 31714–C.

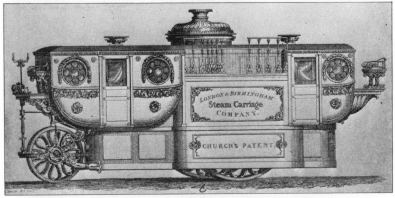

a, Oliver Evans's "Orukter Amphibolos," 1805. Photo of model constructed by Greville
Bathe. Photograph No. 31719–F.

b, Steam vehicle of William Church, 1832. Photograph No. 31719–D.

c, Benz gasoline-powered tricycle, 1885. British Crown copyright. From an exhibit in
the Science Museum, London. Photograph No. 31714–E.

a, Richard Dudgeon's steam vehicle of about 1868.
b, Daimler's first vehicle, 1885, powered with a 1-cylinder, 4-cycle, gasoline engine.

THE CYNOPHERE.

Invented by M. Huret, of Paris, France, and Patented in the United States, December 14, 1875.

The Cynophere consists of two large wheels, between which is a comfortable seat and rest for the feet. In front is a small guide wheel, the direction being controlled at will by a rod held in the right hand, while at the left is a brake by which the speed is regulated. Power is furnished by a dog within each of the side wheels, and so light is the draft that it is no more exertion for the dogs to run upon the treadway of the wheel than it is for them to go at the same speed at their own pleasure. The French Society for the Prevention of Cruelty to Animals, to whom the subject was submitted by the inventor, unanimously endorsed the system.

The vehicle is light and graceful in its mechanism, and can be used by ladies and children, as well as gentlemen, without the slightest danger, discomfort or exertion. For pleasure purposes it is unsurpassed, and when fully introduced to the American public is destined to achieve a popularity far greater than that of the velocipede, while the moderate expense will bring it within the easy reach of all.

Wonder what today's S. P. C. A. would have to say—and the newspapers? Some journals of the '70s seriously commented on the Cynophere advertisement while one suggested that "no respectable canine need take hydrophobia—a new and far more honorable field of operations is open to him if he will but improve the golden opportunity offered by the Cynophere."

ONCE A WONDER.

The first benzine automobile ever built. It was made in 1873 in Vienna by Marcus. Notice the brake on the hind wheel.

This unidentified steam-powered tricycle is one of the oldest automobiles in America. Built in France in 1888, it burns coke and power is transmitted through the single rear wheel.

JAMES STEAM COACH
Built in England in 1829.
Note the steering wheel and the extreme forward position of the driver.
The "Hooter" (England's word for our "horn"), is the real live uniformed
gentleman perched on the seat at extreme rear end. Insignia of the British
Empire on side.

**GORDON
STEAM CARRIAGE**
Built in England in 1829.
The contact on the
ground of the numerous
rods in motion propelled
it.

**TREVITHICK
STEAM
ROAD CARRIAGE**
Built in London, Eng.,
in 1802.

THE NEW PENNINGTON AUTOCAR

1896

This is the machine that so easily beat all comers in the great Motor-Car race which took place in England in May of this year, between Coventry and Birmingham.

The starters in the above race included the De Dion Steam Carriage (winner of the Motor race from Marseilles to Nice this Spring,) and the Panhard-Levassor Vehicle (winner of the great Motor-Car race between Paris and Marseilles); also the winners of all other important Motor races and competitions hitherto held in the world.

The PENNINGTON MOTOR has proved itself to be the Leading Motor in the world, always has been in the front.

For full particulars, address

THE PENNINGTON MOTOR FOREIGN PATENTS SYNDICATE, Ltd.,

5 & 6 Great Winchester Street, LONDON,

Above: 1898 BENZ. Property of Lt. John M. Booth, Colorado Springs, Colo. Took first prize and blue ribbon as oldest car under its own power in Automotive Golden Jubilee Parade at Detroit, June 1946. Single horizontal cylinder; surface carburetor; battery; coil and spark plug ignition; 85-inch wheelbase; sliding gear transmission; driven by 3-inch flat belt from engine; tight and loose pulleys act as clutch; jack shaft and final double chain drive water-cooled with radiator suspended beneath the chassis; no fan; time controls; 6 levers and 3 pedals; steering by center crank on post; car imported from England 1930; engine hand-cranked by pulling spokes of flywheel while using a decompressor; car has been on display in recent years in the Science Building of the Cranbrook School for Boys, Bloomfield Hills, Mich.

Front Wheel Drive

This dog-power fan of 1870 probably had never dreamed of the automobile but he was looking ahead just the same. He thought in terms of three wheels. two under the body and one for driving.

The Thompson Steam Car was the very first all-Australian automobile built in 1896 in Melbourne.

TWO AUSTRALIAN FIRSTS

This is the first Australian built body for a fully enclosed car, designed by James Flood and built by Tarrants about 1907.

First successful petrol-driven Tarrant built in 1898 by the Tarrant Engineering works in South Melbourne. It was sold by D. W. Chandler in 1899. Top speed was 30 to 35 m.p.h.

A Missing Link Vehicle

WHILE French and American motor manufacturers seem bent on eliminating all horse-drawn vehicles, a German inventor, Joseph Vollmer, has evolved a device destined to bridge the gap between the old era and the new. Already his invention has been applied to the postal delivery-wagons of the German Empire; and it is stated that the entire cost of this new government contract has been more than offset to the postal authorities by the great saving of money formerly spent on post-horses. In addition to this there has been a great saving of time in postal deliveries, the newly transformed wagons covering twice their former distances. Now, the device has been patented in this country, and negotiations are being made by several large carriage manufacturers to convert their entire stock of old-fashioned vehicles into automobiles, by the simple substitution of these detachable motors in place of the former front wheels and drivers' boxes. Thus any old stage-coach or horse-drawn four-wheeler can be converted into a motor vehicle, and one and the same motor can be used for different styles of vehicles, such as heavy trucks, delivery-wagons, or pleasure-carriages.

In Germany this new missing link motor is known as the Kuhlstein-Vollmer Motor Vorspann, a word for which there is no exact equivalent in English. Kuhlstein's motors, as used in Hamburg and Berlin, depend on gasoline for their driving-power, since electric charging stations are still too scarce in Germany to make electric motors readily available, but the American patents taken out fully provide for the employment of electric stor-

Vollmer Vorspann.

German Postal Wagon.

age-batteries in similarly constructed motors. The construction of these motors comprises the following elements:

1. A movable axle, which has the two-fold advantage and object of diminishing, as much as possible, the sliding motion necessary for the rotation of the axle, and of rendering the transmission of the motive force upon the axle independent of the various speeds of rotation of the wheel, and this without the use of intermediate gear which it has been necessary to employ hitherto.

2. A coupling mechanism, which effects the engagement of the several mechanisms from the driver's seat, notwithstanding their rotation during turning, as the latter operation is effected by the rotation of the forward section of the vehicle and the engine-box as an entirety.

The invention is illustrated in the accompanying drawings:

Fig. 1 is a side-elevation showing the general arrangement of the forward part of the vehicle, motor mechanism, and housing therefor. Fig. 2 is a cross-section through the same, taken upon the front axle.

Referring to the drawings it will be seen that the whole of the driving-gear is arranged in a rectangular box or housing K, Figs. 1 and 2, situated above the centre of the axle-wheel, the top plate P' of said housing being suspended from the pivot plate P' by means of pivot block S as shown. Said top plate P' forms an integral member with internal teeth, Z, as shown. The pivot block S is rotatably mounted in the hub N of the plate P',

A Missing Link Vehicle

and is retained by nut *m*. Upon the bearing plate P′ is rigidly attached the steering-rod L, served at its upper extremity with a hand-wheel, RX. Said rod terminates at its lower end in a crown wheel, whose teeth mesh with the internal teeth Z of the plate P′. Rollers or balls r are also provided on the bearing surfaces of plates PP′ for the purpose of diminishing friction. In order to decrease sliding motion the differences in the rotation of the wheels upon rounding curves are compensated by means of a differential gear, D, which is mounted directly upon the axle *a* and at one end of the same for economy of space. The differential gear D is situated directly between the two members, a and b, of the driving-axle, and, in order that the latter may form a rigid entirety, the shorter member a is sleeved within the member b as shown in Fig. 2. By this arrangement the axle bearings C are relieved from lateral strain, whilst the provision of an

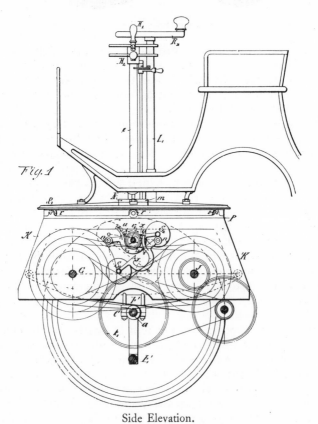

Side Elevation.

intermediate bearing for the separable members a b, such as has hitherto been employed, is rendered unnecessary.

In order that both the springs F, which, it will be observed, carry the housing K, may support an equal load upon the two bearings, C, motion is imparted by means of the chain or gear-wheels k_1 k_2 in such a manner that both act simultaneously upon the bevel pinions w w of differential gear D, which is effected by means of sleeve c, the length of axle b thereby still further obviating any necessity for the provision of an intermediate bearing.

The axle-bearings C are made in two parts, whereby the members a b can be readily inserted. The upper half of the bearings C, which form a strap or staple, are directly connected with the springs F, by which the entire engine-box and forward section of the vehicle are carried. The lower halves of the bearings are connected by means of a bent shaft, E, which imparts the necessary stability to the bearings, and maintains the distance between them always constant. Lubrication is effected by means of annular lubricators, o, served with the lubricant, through suitable ducts as shown.

The parts required for throwing the motor into gear, consisting of tension-pulleys and the requisite operating levers H' H2, are supported upon the top plate P of the engine-box. Through this plate P, at the point where it is pivoted, passes the hollow pivot block S, which extends into the pivot plate P' at its centre, in such a manner that during the turning of the vehicle it is capable of angular displacement, with respect to the plate P. Within said tube are arranged the upright tubes e e' e2 serving to regulate the motive power. The object of this arrangement is, that when the top plate P rotates, the vertical tubes may rotate with it. By this means it is possible to regulate the movement of the under frame, which is itself turning in a very simple manner, whilst the position of the front section, with respect to the vehicle proper, is indicated to the operator.

The vertical tube e' is rigidly connected with the operating lever H2, and the outer tube e2 with the operating lever H2, both said tubes being sleeved in the outer tube or sleeve e, which latter is rigidly fixed in the pivot S of top plate P, and at its upper portion carries the locking disc s of the operating levers. The lower extremities of the tubes ee' are connected with the bevel pinions r' r2, Fig. 2, thereby enabling the shafts v' v2, journaled in the top plate P, to be rotated by turning one of the operating levers H' H2 from o toward o', or from o toward o2, in a right or left-hand direction. The object of this arrange-

A Missing Link Vehicle

ment is, that a pair of tension-pulleys, S′ S2, may be so operated that one of them only (S′ for example) stretches the belt imparting motion to the vehicle, while the other tension-pulleys, S2, remain motionless. The operation and arrangement of the tension-pulley gear with a pair of tension-pulleys, S′ S2, arranged upon the shaft v, are shown in various positions. The two tension pulleys, S′ S2, which are arranged upon levers, pivoted upon opposite points n′n2 upon the top plate, can be disengaged, that is to say, in both cases the toothed pinions z′ z2, mounted upon the shaft v2, are out of engagement with the toothed segments, u, of the tension-pulley levers. In addition to this lever the lower teeth i, of the toothed segments u, are raised a certain distance above the points of the teeth of the segments z′ z2, because the noses x, upon the tension-pulley levers, rest upon the concentric portion of the cam-shaped hubs,

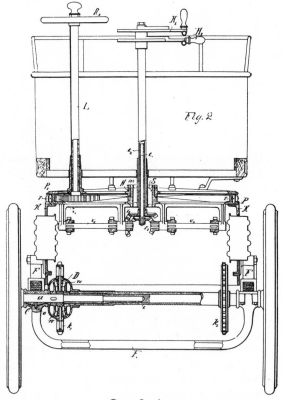

Cross Section.

y, of the toothed pinions z' z2. If the shaft v' is caused to rotate in a left-hand direction (for example) by means of the hand-lever H', the nose x of the tension-pulley S2 falls along the reduced cam-shaped portion of the hub y, and the teeth i gear with teeth z2, thereby displacing the tension-pulley S', which remains stationary, because the nose x continues to slide upon the concentric portion of the hub y and thus experiences no displacement. Only when the operating lever is drawn back does the tension-pulley resume the initial position, and upon continuing to rotate the lever, the tension of pulley S' becomes operative whilst S2 remains stationary. The pair of tension-pulleys

Vollmer Cab.

of the hand-lever H2 act in a similar manner. Motion is effected by means of stepped pulleys G, and J. (Fig. 1.)

In the benzine-motors the vaporizing of the benzine into gas is automatic through a peculiarly constructed carbureter. The carriage can go a speed of twenty miles an hour. The advantage of its construction is that in the speed of the vehicle, the slowest movement can also be obtained, being regulated as desired. The use of fuel is just as high and the same as that of other construction, and the amount of horse-power per hour is 0.6 litre benzine. There is no reason, however, why any other driving-power should not be substituted, since the essentials of the device remain the same.

The "Cyclone Motor"

THE cyclone motor is a two-cylinder petroleum engine cooled by flanges, and making 800 revolutions at the rate of 400 explosions in the cylinder. It is, therefore, not so easily heated as the one-cylinder motors of the same form making 1,200 revolutions and more per minute. Of the two sizes in which the motor is made, the one develops 135 kilogram-meters (975.105 foot pounds) of energy, and weighs 32 kilograms (2.2 pounds to the kilogram) with the fly-wheel; and the other develops 200 kilogram-meters (1,446.60 foot pounds) of energy at 800 revolutions, and weighs but 50 kilograms approximately.

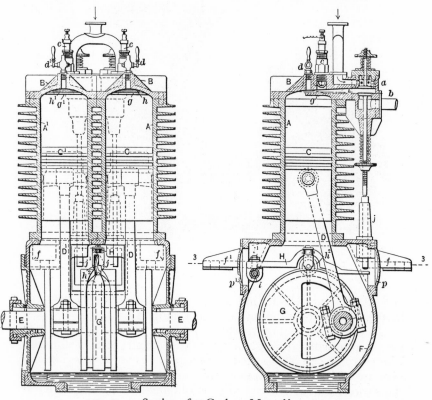

FIG. 1   Section of " Cyclone Motor "   FIG. 2

In Figure 1, A and A' are two vertical cylinders arranged side by side and provided with heads B and B', each having an automatic admission valve a and an escape valve d, controlled by

The Automobile Magazine

means which will be later described. The igniters are represented by c, c', and the cocks controlling the compression by d d'. The pistons are of the single-acting type, and are connected by rods with the shaft E. The lower portion of the operating mechanism is inclosed in a casing F, on which the cylinders are secured. The motor is fastened in position by the shoes ff.

At the upper portion of each cylinder is a partition g, which serves to deflect the fresh gases admitted through the valve a and prevents mingling with residual gases near the igniters.

One of the novel features of this motor is the method employed for controlling the escape valves b b'. A cam G is keyed on the crank of the shaft E (between the two piston rods D D') and turns therewith. The periphery of this cam is formed with two grooves intersecting at x (Figure 3).

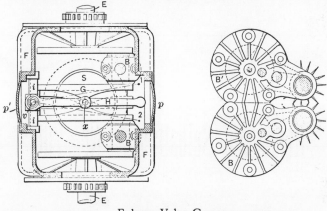

FIG. 3   Exhaust Valve Governor   FIG. 4

At the upper part of this cam is a roller h engaging the groove and journalled in a lever H (Figure 2), fulcrumed at i i.

The lever has both vertical and horizontal movement, the latter being due to the peculiar 8-shape of the groove. When the lever is shifted horizontally, its flattened free end alternately moves to the extreme points indicated by the numerals 1 and 2 (Figure 3). In these two positions the lever is given a vertical movement by the cam by which the stems j j' of the escape valves b b are alternately elevated. The reseating of the valves b b is effected by a spring, the tension of which can be regulated by means of a collar screwing upon the stem. The two pistons, in response to the movements of the single crank of the shaft E will always act together. As the cycles alternate, the motor shaft will be driven at a uniform rate of speed.

Hammonia Motor-Dreirad

mit Rücksitz.

1901

Hammonia-Selbstfahrer Nr. 700.

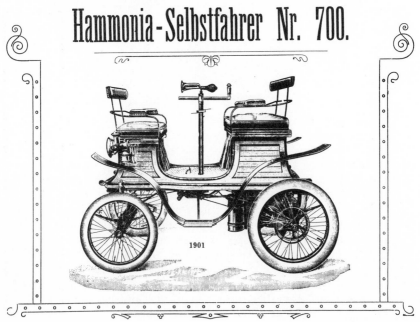

1901

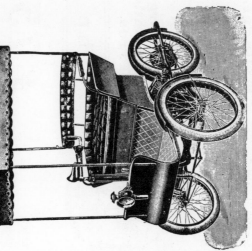

WOLF MOTETTE.

1903

Water Cooled Cylinder.

Free Engine.

Chain Driven.

Extra Large Pneumatic Tyres.

$3\frac{1}{2}$ h.p.

Price: **£75.**

Fitted with Starting Handle, enabling the rider to start the motor before mounting machine.

Wearwell Motor Carriage Co., Limited., Wolverhampton.

Send for Lists.   ∅ ∅   London Agents: COX & CO., 62, Holborn Viaduct.

The Stirling Dogcart.

1903

The 'Canterbury' Car.

Price, 178 Guineas.

"The Almost Silent Car."

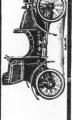

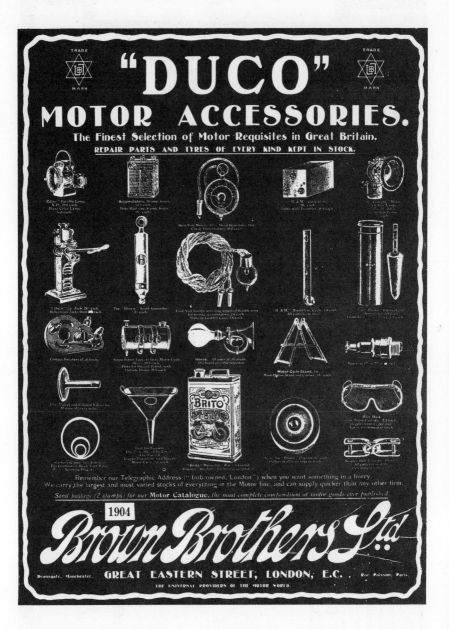

48

49

DARRACQ
THE CAR THAT LEADS THEM ALL

Holder of More Records Than Any Other Car in the World

8, 9, 10, 12, 20 & 24 Horse Power

ALSO DELIVERY WAGONS : : : : : : ACCESSORIES CONSTANTLY ON HAND

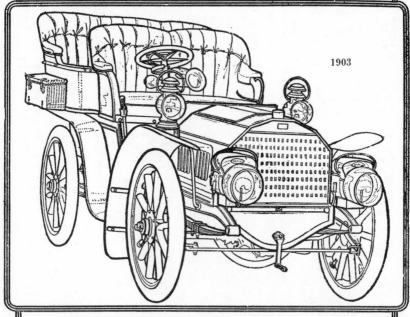

1903

Every Modern Improvement, Luxuriously Upholstered, Good in All Weathers, Exceptional Hill Climbers, Frame of Specially Made Cut Channel Steel (no wood). ❡ One of these cars selected and purchased last week for King Edward VII. ❡ Three-fourths of imported cars sold in the United States are *DARRACQS* and sold through us

IMMEDIATE DELIVERY

American Darracq Automobile Company

CONTROLLED BY F. A. LA ROCHE COMPANY
SOLE AMERICAN IMPORTERS & DISTRIBUTORS | 652-664 Hudson Street, NEW YORK

BRANCHES { CHICAGO 501-4 Wabash Ave.   PHILADELPHIA 262 No. Broad St.   PITTSBURG 3994 Forbes St.   NEW YORK 147 West 38th St.

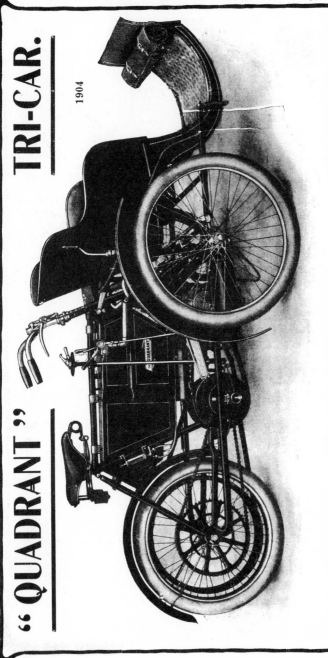

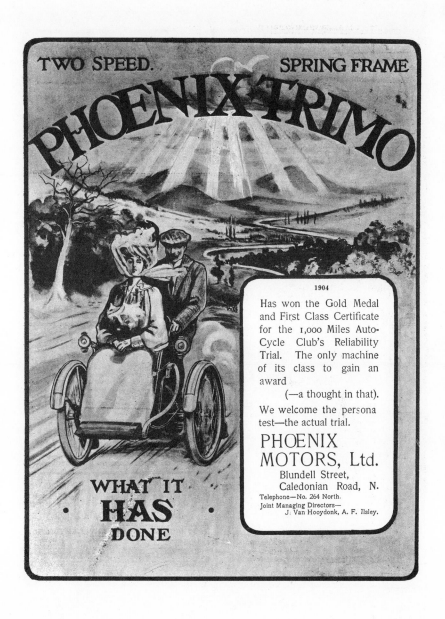

TWO SPEED.   SPRING FRAME

PHOENIX TRIMO

1904

Has won the Gold Medal and First Class Certificate for the 1,000 Miles Auto-Cycle Club's Reliability Trial. The only machine of its class to gain an award

(—a thought in that).

We welcome the persona test—the actual trial.

PHOENIX MOTORS, Ltd.

Blundell Street,
Caledonian Road, N.

Telephone—No. 264 North.
Joint Managing Directors—
J. Van Hooydonk, A. F. Ilsley.

WHAT IT
HAS
DONE

HUMBER MOTORS

1904

THE MOTOR BICYCLE

pronounced by experts to be "in all the world unequalled." The pioneer of the Chain-drive, perfectly balanced mo or, obtained by a centrally placed engine. Holds World's Speed Records, Gold Medals for Reliability and Excellence of design.

Prices from 40 Guineas.

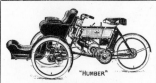

THE HUMBER OLYMPIA

fills the want between the Motor Bicycle and Car. Seating two persons, with exceptional comfort for the passenger in the fore-car, taking up less space than a car, and costing less for up-keep. Water-cooled, Free Engine, Two Speeds.

Prices £85 and £90.

The HUMBERETTE

is a reliable little runabout, eminently adapted for use by professional and business men.

As an official proof of its excellence, it gained the Automobile Club's Certificate for Reliability.

Prices: 5 h.p., 125 and 140 Guineas.   **6½ h.p., 150 and 160 Guineas.**

 We have several bargains in second-hand Motor Cycles and Humberettes.   **Write for Particulars.**

Catalogue and Complete Car Specification sent free on application.

HUMBER LIMITED, Beeston (Notts), & Coventry.

London Motor Cycle Depot: 32, Holborn Viaduct, London, E.C.
Car Show Rooms & Garage: 13, Cambridge Place, Paddington, W.

LIVERPOOL—73, Bold Street.   BIRMINGHAM—4, Victoria Square.   SOUTHAMPTON—27, London Road.
MANCHESTER—5, Deansgate.   NOTTINGHAM—19, Wheelergate.   STOURBRIDGE—Oldswinford.

No. 323.

The latest arrival is "HORBICK MINOR."

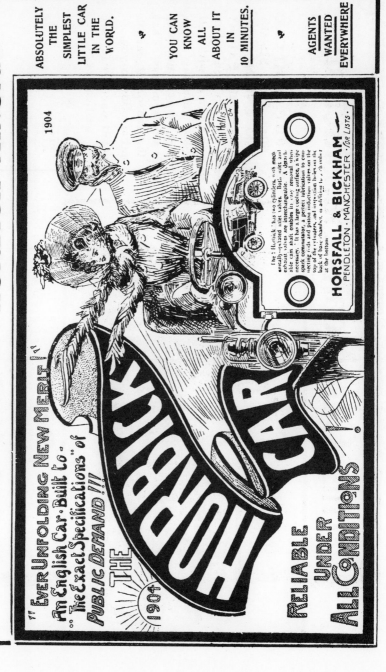

"EVER UNFOLDING NEW MERIT!"
An English Car Built to
"The Exact Specifications of
PUBLIC DEMAND!!!

THE HORBICK CAR

1904

RELIABLE UNDER ALL CONDITIONS

The Horbick has two cylinders, with mechanically-operated inlet valves. Both inlet and exhaust valves are interchangeable. A considerable cam shaft enables its easy removal when necessary. It has a large cooling surface, a wipe spark commutator, a perfect lubrication to connecting rods and piston induction valves on the top of the cylinders, and inspection holes on the back of base chamber, in addition to a chamber at the bottom

HORSFALL & BICKHAM
PENDLETON · MANCHESTER · for lists

Will Hollis '04

56

MARVELLOUS VALUE.

1904

"The BROWN"
8 H.P. SINGLE-CYLINDER
CAR.

Such is the opinion of everyone who has inspected this wonderful little Car, which is equipped with every modern improvement, and is, without any exception, the most up-to-date small Car yet placed on the market.

£175.

"BROWN" 8 h.p. Gear Driven CAR

READ THE SPECIFICATION.

Motor.—8 h.p. Single cylinder, vertical, fitted with a Governor, 110 m/m bore, 120 m/m stroke, 12,000 to 15,000 revolutions per minute. The Governor gear is enclosed in oil-tight case.

Ignition.—Electric "Wipe Spark" Contact Breaker, Trembler Coil, Switch, &c.

Frame.—Wood, strengthened with flitch plates, extra long springs.

Transmission.—Three Speeds and Reverse (direct drive on top speed) actuated by a single change speed lever (7, 17 and 28 miles per hour). The Gear Box is fitted with plain gun-metal bushes with ball thrusts at either end of the shafts, provision for ample lubrication of the bushes being made. A Cardan Shaft of improved design is employed for transmitting the power from the gear box to the rear live axle. The teeth on the driving and bevel pinions are of a large pitch, and the driving pinion is fitted with a ball thrust and runs in a long plain bearing. The live axle is well balanced and runs on ½ in. balls, special provision being made for easy adjustment. The clutch, which is an internal cone, can be easily removed without touching the engine or gear box.

Lubrication.—The Gear Box and Rear Axle being oil tight only require filling occasionally, and are so constructed that all bushes and bearings receive ample lubrication. A combined force and drip lubricator is fitted to the dashboard, one lead going to the plain bearing of the bevel driving pinion and another to the engine crank case. Special means are provided for lubricating the Cardan shaft joints, which will only require occasional attention.

Petrol Tank.—Has a capacity of four gallons.

The Water Circulation is maintained by a **Gear Driven Pump** attached to the front of the engine in an easily accessible position, which can be entirely detached by the removal of one nut. An exceedingly efficient honeycomb type radiator is fitted. This does away with the necessity of a water tank and its many troublesome connections.

Brakes.—These are of the metal to metal type, made in two halves; the one on the counter-shaft is applied by one foot pedal only, the other foot pedal operates the clutch only. The brakes on the rear wheels, which are of special design, are applied by a side lever. Either brake will hold the car independently, backwards or forwards, on the steepest gradient.

Wheels.—Wood, artillery type, equal size, 30 × 3¼ in., fitted with Continental or Dunlop tyres.

Levers.—The Change Speed and Brake Levers are conveniently placed, the advance spark and accelerator levers are fixed to the steering pillar within easy reach of the hand. The two latter levers are fitted with Bowden mechanism, as also is the air regulator to the carburetter which is attached to the dashboard.

Length of Wheel Base, 6 ft., extreme width, 4 ft. 10 in. Supplied complete with two side lamps, horn and set of tools.

Trial Runs on application.   *Easy Payments arranged.*   *Write for Motor Vehicle List.*

BROWN BROTHERS, LTD.,

West End Showroom - - 15, Newman Street, Oxford Street, London, W.
Head Office - - - - - Great Eastern Street, London, E.C.

MANCHESTER—269-273, Deansgate.   PARIS—31, Rue de la Folie Mericourt.

B.K.

FOR ALL MOTOR ACCESSORIES
Obtainable from all Agents.
Special Terms to Shippers and Large Buyers.

B.K.

THE B.K. AUTO-TREMBLER.

For converting non-trembling into trembling coils. Makes starting easy. Misfires impossible. No alteration at Contact breaker is necessary.

Size, 5 in. x 3 in. x 2 in.

Price 18/6 each

MULTIPLE TOOL.

As supplied in the Minerva Sets: also Humber Motor Cycle.

Contains 10 Different Tools in the Handle.

Price 1/6 each.   Postage 3d.

The B.K. HANDLEBAR SWITCH.

Designed for momentary or permanent interruption. Well and strongly made, Neat and nicely finished.
Price **5/-** each.

NEW TWO-WAY SWITCH.

To fit on Top Tube. Price **4/-** each.

B.K. HIGH SPEED COILS.

1904

Fitted with new High Speed Trembler, working up to **6,000** revs. per minute.
We have sold HUNDREDS without a single complaint.

PRICE—

No. 4. For Motor Cycles, size over terminals, 6 x 4 x 2¾ in. ... **32/-** each.
No. 5. For Voiturettes, size over terminals, 7½ x 5 x 3½ in. ... **40/-** each.

PORCELAINS.

For Repairing Sparking Plugs
Price **8d.** each

INSULATED WIRES.

Low Tension Wire.
No. 11. Double Insulation ... ... **5d.** yard
High Tension Wire.
No. 15. Triple Insulation, diameter 9 m/m **1/4** „
„ 16. „ „ „ 12 m/m **2/4** „
„ 17. „ „ „ 15 m/m **3/-** „

LONGUEMARE CARBURETTERS.

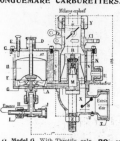

No. 41. Model G. With Throttle, only **20/-** each
No. 48. Model E. With Throttle and Regulator ... ... **32/-** „
No. 54. Model H. Ditto... ... ... **48/-** „

THE BEST MOTOR CYCLE TOOL BAG

No. 12.—Solid leather, with divisions for tools and spare parts, **8/-** each.

THE B.K. MOTOR EYE GUARD.

Bound with Silk only. **8d.**
Bound with Silk and Chenille, **1/-**.

Transparent Celluloid.

B.K. MICA SPARKING PLUG.

No. 25—Mica Insulation Brass Fittings **4/-** each.

LEATHER CAITERS.

For Temporary Repairs of Outer Covers of Tyres.

No. 15. For Tyres on Wood Rims—
65 m m. 80 or 85 m/n. 90 m/m. 120 m/m.
3/2 **3/8** **4/6** **5/2** each
No. 16. For Tyres on Metal Rims—
2/7 **2/10** **3/1**
Wire cable for fixing above, **2d.** per yard.
An effective means of temporarily repairing gashed or cut outer covers. Indispensable for touring.

BRANSOM, KENT & CO., Ltd., LONDON, 332, Goswell Rd., E.C. & PARIS, 1, Rue Torricelli.

Telegrams 9085 London Wall.   Telegrams: "Cycladatus, London"

The GILBURT LIGHT CAR.

1905

Two Cylinders 6 h.p.

Price—
Two Seats £125
Three ,, £130

Engine	6 h.p., two cylinder, vertical.
Bore and Stroke	75 mm by 80 mm.
Ignition	High tension
No of speeds...	Three and reverse.
Gearing	Sliding spur wheels, direct drive on top speed.
Transmission ...	By chains.
Cooling	Pump on cam shaft and radiators.
Frame	Weldless steel tube.
Brakes	Two double-acting, foot & hand lever.
Wheels	Artillery, 26-in.
Tyres	Pneumatic, 2½-in. Palmer or Continental
Wheel-base ...	5 ft. 9in.
Weight	7 cwt.
Upholstered in real Leather.	

This elegant and attractive Car has been designed and constructed to meet the growing demand for a reliable Light Car at a moderate price, which, while capable of long distance journeys, is at the same time easy to drive, under perfect control, fast and reliable and a powerful Hill Climber.

It is the outcome of practical experiments, and the builder offers it to the public with the fullest confidence as to its capabilities, no trouble or expense having been spared in the design or construction.

Among other advantages, the following are claimed:—

Smooth and Easy Running, with absence of Vibration;
Silence in Working;
Hill Climbing Capacity;
Simplicity of Construction and Ease of Control.
Reliability.

Guaranteed against Faulty Workmanship for six months.

TRIAL RUNS GIVEN.

E. A. GILBURT,

80a, Salusbury Road, West Kilburn, N.W.

Telephone, 689 P.O. Hampstead.

READER?

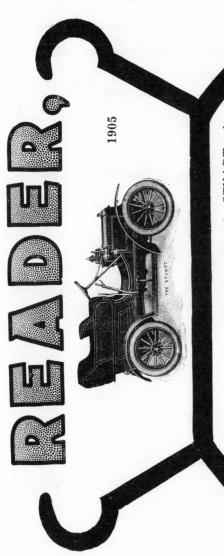

1905

THE STUART

the Press and Public alike acknowledge the STUART to be of wonderful value. Personally we have full confidence in your finding it to be the ideal little car your fancy doubtless often pictures.—It is a small car which can be relied upon in all capacities. It will be ready for a spin whenever you are inclined, and it is wonderfully responsive to the man at the wheel, climbs hills with greatest ease, and affords maximum enjoyment with low cost of purchase and upkeep. To the man with a moderately full, but not a fat pocket-book, it should strongly appeal. It has 7 h.p. 2-cylinder, governed engine, 3 speeds (forward and reverse), artillery wheels, live axle with Cardan shaft drive.

PRICES: **2 seats, £165. 3 seats £180. 4 seats, £190.**

SEND FOR LIST "A" TO—

STAR CYCLE Co. Ltd., Wolverhampton.

Motor Cars
FOR MEDICAL MEN.

Dr. ——, of Much Wenlock, Salop, writes thus about his

—— HUMBER FOUR-CYLINDER CAR. ——

"As I believe you supplied me with one of your first Four-Cylinder Light Cars, I think it only fair to write and say how pleased I am with it. I have had the car in constant use day and night for three weeks, and during that time have driven it about six or seven hundred miles over bad and very hilly roads. In my o_inion it is an ideal car for a medical man, as it is very silent, and even in a hilly country like this, one has seldom to get off the high gear. Another great point in its favour to a medical man is the ease in starting, as I find that even after a long wait at a patient's house the car will start 'on the switch' nine times out of ten. During the three months I have had the car I have not had the slightest trouble with it ; the only adjustment I have had to do was to tighten up the pump chain."

1905

Price.
385
Gns.

Price,
385
Gns.

"HUMBER"

COMPLETE SPECIFICATION ON APPLICATION.

OTHER MODELS.

7½ h.p. Royal Humberette - - - -	**200** Gns.
8-10 h.p. Four-Cylinder Coventry Light Car -	**225** ,,
8-10 h.p. Four-Cylinder Beeston Humber Car -	**300** ,,
10-12 h.p. Beeston Humber Light Car - -	**300** ,,
16-20 h.p. Four-Cylinder Beeston Humber Car -	**450** ,,

HUMBER, LTD. Works : Beeston (Notts.) & Coventry.

66

The Reliable RILEY

1905
TRI-CAR

secured **1st Class** Certificate in the recent A. C. C. Six Days' Reliability Trials.

You really ought to get particulars of the new Riley Tri-car de Luxe, 6 and 9 h.p. A glance at its specification will convince you that it is undoubtedly **THE Tri-car de Luxe**, while an extended trial will thoroughly satisfy you as far as comfort, speed, and hill-climbing are concerned.

Early delivery of 1906 Models can now be arranged.

RILEY CYCLE Co., Ld.,
City Works, Coventry.

The Phoenix Wallaroo Quadcar in

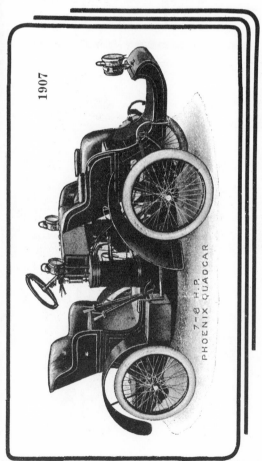

1907

7-8 H.P.
PHŒNIX QUADCAR

21st January, 1907.

"The Quadcar landed in Adelaide on the 17th December. I took delivery on the 19th. We gave her a trial trip to Mount Lofty—a good test for hill-climbing. On the 20th I drove her to Wallaroo, a distance of 100 miles, and I can only say she gave every satisfaction. I have done already nearly 800 miles, and all I can add is that as far as comfortable riding is concerned the Quadcar is first class—it is a good hill-climber and a fast machine."

R. BURDEN,
Wallaroo, South Australia.

The Phœnix Quadcar is giving satisfaction all over the world. In buying a Phœnix Quadcar you buy the result of 5 years' experience in light passenger machines. Price **£115** nett. Magneto, £8 : 8 extra. Prompt delivery. Lists by return.

PHŒNIX MOTORS, Ltd., Blundell St., Caledonian Road, N.

Telephone 264 North. Joint Managing Directors: J. VAN HOOYDONK and A. F. ILSLEY. GRADUAL PAYMENT TERMS ARRANGED

Agents for Quadcar for Lancashire and Cheshire—The Addison Motor Co., 18–20, Addison Street, Liverpool.

"The Most Efficient Car on the Road."

THE NEW   1906

Arrol-Johnston

The New Arrol-Johnston 12-15 h.p. Tonneau.

The Winner of the Tourist Trophy Race, and other Important and Varied Contests.

WE SHALL BE EXHIBITING AT THE GLASGOW SHOW.

Agents in Districts in which we are not already represented are invited to communicate with us.

Please send for Catalogue Number 14.

The New Arrol-Johnston Car Company, Ltd.
PAISLEY, SCOTLAND.

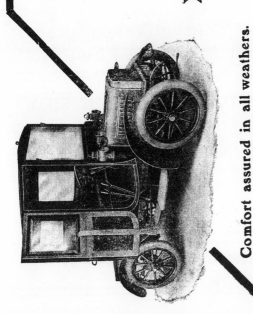

ANY *CAR CAN*
══ *CRAWL*
UP A HILL
fitted with a low gear of 6 to 8 miles per hour.

Remember that the

Remarkable

Records of the 20 h.p.

ROLLS-

ROYCE in

Rushing up the steepest

Roof-like gradients kindly selected by

Readers of "The Motor" are made with a gear-

Ratio which at 1,000

Revolutions of the motor per minute gives

1906

15 miles per hour on the lowest gear and
50 miles per hour on the highest gear.

PLEASE WRITE FOR TRIAL RUN.

C. S. ROLLS & CO.,

74

JACKSONS

1907

fitted with De Dions, give complete satisfaction. 100 unsolicited Testimonials may be seen at our offices. WE PRODUCE THE LARGEST VARIETY of Light Cars in the world at £130, £165, £175, £195, £210, £225, £235, £260, £400.

ONE-CYLINDER JACKSONS ... from £130
TWO   ,,   ...   ,,   £210
FOUR   ,,   ...   ,,   £260

No. 6 JACKSON, £235.

No. 4S JACKSON, £225.
Testimonials.

I have travelled about 12,000 miles on my Jackson, and am delighted with the car in every way, etc.
(Dr.) G. STUART MOORE.

My Jackson Car still goes as well as ever; has been in use all winter, and has not cost me sixpence in repairs, etc.
(Major) N. BARTON.

The Jackson has behaved splendidly in the deep snow and frost. I have run it now 3,650 miles.
(Rev.) ARTHUR WILSON.

I am glad to tell you that after two years' hard work I have examined the engine, gear box, and differential of my 6 h.p. Jackson Dogcart, and find all the working parts in perfect condition. I have not had a single breakdown, etc.
C. E. MALONEY.

I have travelled 16,000 miles, fulfilling 360 engagements, failing once only through the accumulator running down, etc.
WALTER GRAHAM (The Human Marionette).

My Jackson has been running very satisfactorily, etc.
(Rev.) J. H. G. RANDOLPH.

Its hill-climbing powers are wonderful, etc.
(Rev.) B. W. BRADFORD.

I have now had my Jackson Dogcart for some little time, and am more than pleased with it, etc. GEO. W. FRANCIS, M.B., C.M., L.M.
(Dr.)

R. REYNOLD JACKSON & CO., Ltd., 13, High St., Notting Hill Gate, LONDON, W.

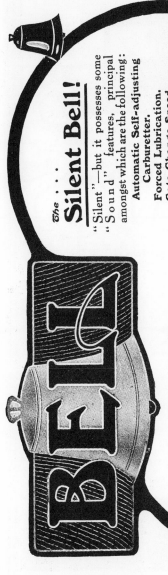

IRIS CARS

1907

The Iris is of "SOUND CONSTRUCTION and GOOD DESIGN" (vide Motor News). These **TWO ESSENTIAL POINTS** being the key to the well-known

SILENCE, RELIABILITY,
SIMPLICITY, FLEXIBILITY,
of the

I R I S

Reliability fully tested in Irish Reliability Trials—an absolute non-stop run being made. Last year also **full marks** were obtained for Reliability in the Scottish Trials.

Full particulars will be sent on request.
We shall be pleased to arrange a practical trial without obligation to purchase.

CHASSIS PRICES.
25 h.p., complete with Tyres   -   -   £575
35 h.p..,   "   "   -   -   £700
40 h.p., 6 cylinders, complete with Tyres £875

IRIS CARS, LTD., 7, 8 & 9, BIRD STREET
(Adjoining "The Times" Book Club),
OXFORD STREET, LONDON, W.
Telegrams: "Cirisars, London."   Tel. 1687, Paddington.
Agents for Glasgow & West of Scotland :—The Glasgow Automobile Co., Ltd., West George Street, Glasgow.

R.T. LANG

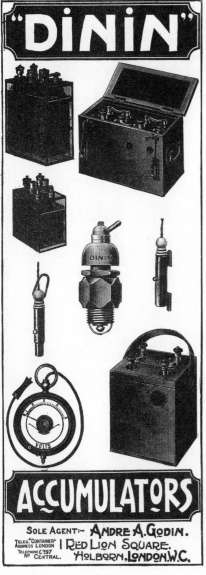
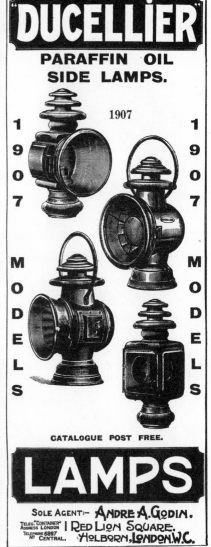

84

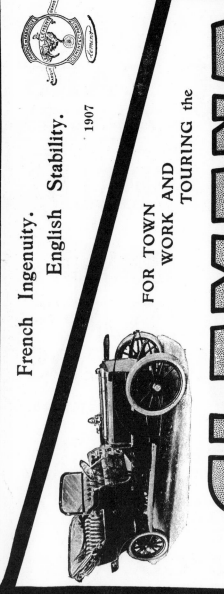

88

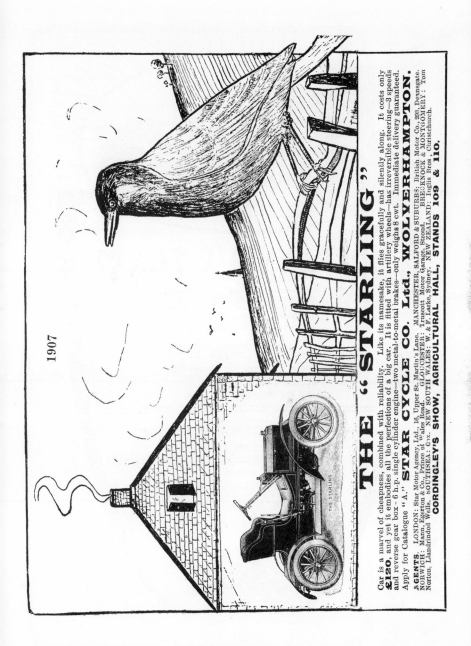

1907

THE "STARLING"

Car is a marvel of cheapness, combined with reliability. Like its namesake, it flies gracefully and silently along. It costs only £120, and yet it embodies all the perfections of a big car. It is fitted with artillery wheels—has irreversible steering—3 speeds and reverse gear box - 6 h.p. single cylinder engine—two metal-to-metal brakes—only weighs 8 cwt. Immediate delivery guaranteed. Apply for Catalogue "A." STAR CYCLE CO. Ltd., WOLVERHAMPTON.

AGENTS. LONDON: Star Motor Agency, Ltd., 16, Upper St. Martin's Lane. MANCHESTER, SALFORD & SUBURBS: British Motor Co., 208, Deansgate. NORWICH: Mann, Egerton & Co., Prince of Wales Road. GLOUCESTER: Truscott Motor Garage, Stroud. BRECKNOCK & MONTGOMERY: Tom Norton, Llandrindod Wells. SOUTHSEA: Ox. NEW SOUTH WALES: W. & F. Larke, Sydney. NEW ZEALAND: Inglis Bros., Christchurch.
CORDINGLEY'S SHOW, AGRICULTURAL HALL, STANDS 109 & 110.

10 h.p. CAR, £285

(can be fitted with live axle if desired).

BRITANNIA'S TOAST

Britannia's voice rings over the sea,
Here's to the kingly car,
Here's to the motor, speedy and free,
The honest, reliable Star."

1907

Every part is of Britain's best,
Wrought with the greatest care,
By my sturdy sons with skill and zest,
Till the car is of beauty rare.

And as you speed over hill and dale,
Till the sun grows dim and dies,
You will agree in exultant glee,
That the Star is indeed a prize.

Send for List C,

STAR ENGINEERING Co.,
WOLVERHAMPTON.

Agents :—

LONDON : Star Motor Agency, Ltd,, 16, Upper St, Martins Lane,
LIVERPOOL; Wooler Bros., Sefton Motor Garage, 59, Lark Lane.
LEEDS: J. Wales Smith, 12, Rampart Road, Woodhouse.
STOCKPORT : J. Garlick Looker, Portland Grove, Heaton Moor.
BIRMINGHAM : Newey's Motor Co., Station Street.
BELFAST ; Northern Motor Co., 38, Chichester Street.
DUBLIN : Turner Bros., Ltd., 104, Gt. Brunswick Street.

Exhibiting Cars at the Olympia Show (Commerial Vehicles),
March 7th to 16th,   Stand No. 32.

1907

18 H.P. REO

With luxurious Semi-tulip Side Entrance Bodies;
BEST ENGLISH COACHWORK,
complete with hood, lamps, and full equipment,

————£320————

DELIVERIES now guaranteed 7 days from date of order.

18 h.p. **REO Landaulette, complete** - **£360**
10 h.p. **REO 4 Seats, complete** - - **£165**

Absolute Silence. No Vibration, Marvellous Flexibility, Lasting Reliability, Highest Grade
Workmanship, Best Materials Obtainable, Hill Climbing Extraordinary.

FULL GUARANTEE FOR 12 MONTHS.
Write for particulars.   Trial runs free.

REO MOTORS LTD.,

BROAD SANCTUARY,   WESTMINSTER,
(Opposite the Abbey and)   **LONDON, S.W.**
(Houses of Parliament.)

Telegrams; "JELAMCO, LONDON."   Telephone No. 59 WESTMINSTER.

English body on U.S. -built Reo

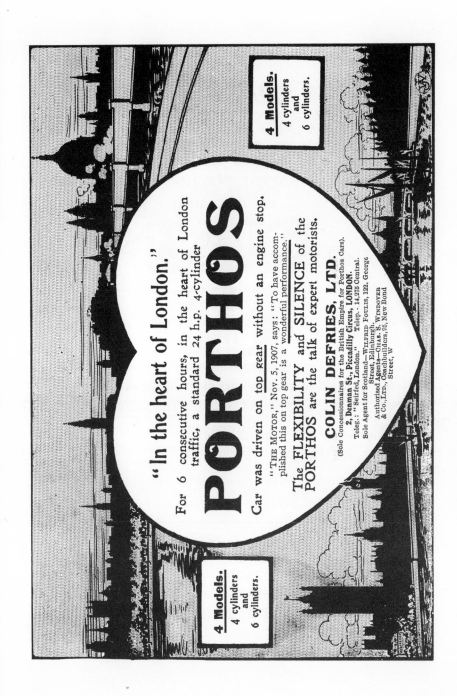

Il Pneumatico MICHELIN

HA VINTO LE ROTAIE!

1906

Circuito delle Ardenne — Heath percorre 600 km. in ore 7 e 30'.
Coppa Florio — Brescia — Matteo Ceirano compie 300 Km. in ore 2 40' 48".

LE PNEU MICHELIN A VAINCU LE RAIL

HEATH SUR VOITURE PANHARD BAT DE 30 MINUTES SUR 600 KILOMETRES LE TRAIN LE PLUS RAPIDE DU MONDE

Coppa Vanderbilt — Lancia percorre 300 Km. in ore 2 e 39'.
L'espresso Parigi-Calais, il treno più rapido del mondo percorre 300 Km. in ore 3 20', e 600 Km. (andata e ritorno) in ore 7.

Agenzia Italiana Pneus Michelin

MILANO - 67, Foro Bonaparte

FABBRICA AUTOMOBILI

ISOTTA FRASCHINI

SOCIETÀ ANONIMA CON SEDE IN MILANO

Capitale L. 1.500.000 interamente versato

Stabilimento ed Uffici - MILANO - Via Monte Rosa, N. 79

Landaulet "Isotta Fraschini,, modello 1906 3 posti interni, 2 esterni

MODELLI 1906

$^{16}|_{22}$ HP - $^{28}|_{35}$ HP - $^{50}|_{65}$ HP.

Chassis - Vetture - Omnibus

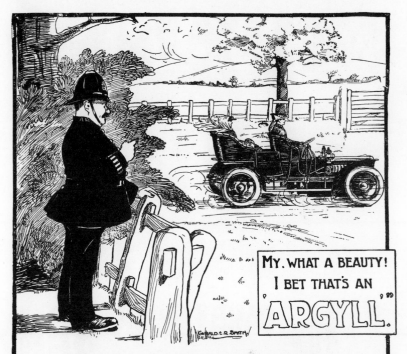

MY. WHAT A BEAUTY!
I BET THAT'S AN
ARGYLL.

The elegant and handsome bodies of the Argyll Cars are well in keeping with that perfection of mechanism which has made the reputation of

The FAMOUS ARGYLL. 1906

Made only from the best selected materials, finished in the highest class style, and upholstered in leather and best quality horsehair, they present a perfect example of the coach-builder's craft. ———————————————

Over a dozen types of bodies are made, amongst which the most fastidious will have no
difficulty in making a satisfactory choice. ————————

ARGYLL MOTORS, Ld., ALEXANDRIA, by GLASGOW.

London Agents: ARGYLLS, LONDON, LTD., 17, Newman Street, Oxford Street, W.

'ADAMS'

1907

10 H.P.
CARRY FOUR
or
CARRY TWO
£ 250

Fitted with Detachable Seats and Side Doors, and Full Accessories.

PEDALS TO PUSH
THAT'S ALL.

We also give you our REMARKABLE FREE REPAIR BOND, which protects you in addition to the usual Maker's Guarantee.

ADAMS MANUFACTURING CO., Ltd.,

Works: BEDFORD.   **106, NEW BOND STREET, W.**

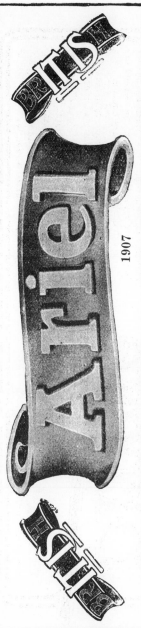

Ariel 1907

BRITISH BUILT

GOLD MEDAL IN THE SCOTTISH TRIALS,

ALSO

— 11 Firsts in Hill Climbs out of Possible 12 —

AND

Highest Aggregate of Marks irrespective of Class.

Any make of car taken in part payment.

TRIAL RUNS ARRANGED.

Please send for Catalogue, or call and inspect our

UP-TO-DATE MODELS.

Head Office and Show-rooms: **ARIEL MOTORS, Ltd.,** 101, New Bond Street, London, W.

"I run on for ever."

THE SIX-CYLINDER Brooke

1907

Brooke

Telephone: 3503 MAYFAIR.
Telegrams: "BROOKDOM, LONDON."

Have a free trial run on the Brooke;
we shall be pleased to arrange it.

DESERVES YOUR ATTENTION

because it is a very high class six-cylinder automobile, handsome in appearance, perfect in engineering, and its price is not beyond the reach of the man of moderate means.

Look at the list of Brooke prices, compare them with the average price of four-cylinder cars.

30 h.p., six-cylinder model, chassis, **£685.**
Side-entrance, **£750.**
Landaulette, **£820.**

BROOKE MOTORS (London), LTD.,
35, Albemarle Street, W.

A.J.W"

The two leaders—official and social—in the King's Indian Empire

select the SIX-CYLINDER

LONDON MADE NAPIER

The original and still the best.

Photo by Elliott and Fry.

His Excellency The Viceroy of India, requiring a motor car for use in his official duties, naturally ordered a six-cylinder Napier as being the embodiment of the finest engineering skill, as well as holding the position of the leading British motor car. His Excellency would not be satisfied with anything but the best.

1907

His Highness The Nizam of Hyderabad, after testing many of the leading British and Foreign motor cars, selected the six-cylinder Napier, as being most satisfactory in every respect. One Napier Limousine for His Highness's personal use, two Zenana Napier Carriages for his ladies, and three Napier Touring Cars for his staff have been already delivered, and further cars are in the course of construction.

Photo by Illustrations Bureau.

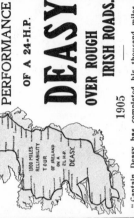

THE SHREWD AGENT is fixing
The Rover Cab Agency

1907

THE ROVER STATION CAB.

Because these Cabs
are suitable for
Doctors,
Professional Men,
Cab Proprietors,
Job Masters,
Hotel Proprietors,
and all kinds of buyers
and hirers.

Chassis, with
tyres and
non-skid band,

£280

Complete Cab,
either model,

£350

With taximeter,
£375.

THE ROVER LANDAULETTE CAB.

Rover Quality.   Rover Prices.
British Manufacture Throughout.

Buy a car with
a good reputation.

The car with the
unequalled record—

De Dion Bouton

The Reliable and Durable Car.   1906

Undoubtedly the best guide to the prospective buyer of a car is its reputation. It affords the best and only definite reasons to justify its consideration, while the reliability of its running, durability of working parts and maintenance cost, are actual existing facts—not the unknown quantities of a cheap and untried car.

When the purchaser of a low-priced or unknown car finds, after a few weeks' running, that it requires considerable adjustment, necessitating frequent visits to repair shops, and the constant expenditure of money, the fallacy of buying a car of second-rate quality, merely because it was low in first cost, becomes very obvious.

De Dion Bouton Cars have for years been known to be the most reliable, most durable, and most economical—therefore the least expensive.

Full particulars of all models on request.

New models, 8 h.p., 10 h.p., 12-14 h.p., 18 h.p., and 30 h.p.

De Dion Bouton (1907), Ltd.,

Sole Authorised Representatives of Messrs.
De Dion Bouton et Cie., of Puteaux, France,
for the United Kingdom and all British Colonies
and Dependencies,

**10, Gt. Marlborough Street,
Regent Street, London, W.**

Telegrams—"Andesite, London."
Telephone—Nos. 8160 & 8161 Central.

½-gal. 1/6
¼-gal. 2/6

1-gal. 5/-
4-gals. 17/6

Why purchase a first-class car and ruin its mechanism

by the use of inferior oil?

De Dion Bouton Oil

is the result of a long series of tests and experiments to discover the best lubricating oil for motors, and its consistent quality is guaranteed by frequent analysis by the chemists of the De Dion Bouton factory.

Booklet, containing illustrations and full particulars of De Dion accessories, free.

De Dion Bouton (1907), Ltd.

Address as above.

A.J.W.

F·I·A·T

❡ The recent victories gained by F.I.A.T. Cars over representative makes of all nationalities in the three greatest events of the year—**The Targa Florio, Kaiser's Cup, and Grand Prix**—afford substantial proof of the merits of excellent workmanship of these increasingly popular cars.

1907

Various types of Touring Cars and Automobiles de Luxe for immediate and early delivery.

FIAT MOTORS, Ltd.,
37-38, LONG ACRE,
LONDON, W.C.

Telephones: 7947 Gerrard (3 lines).
Telegrams: " Fiatism, London."

SIMPLE,
DURABLE and
RELIABLE.

A FEW SECOND-HAND CARS FOR DISPOSAL.

We have a few Second-hand F.I.A.T. Cars in stock, which have been taken in part exchange for newer types or higher powered models of the same make. All these have been thoroughly overhauled, and are guaranteed in first-class order and condition. A splendid opportunity of acquiring a high grade car in perfect order at a most reasonable price.

For prices and particulars write or call at the above address.

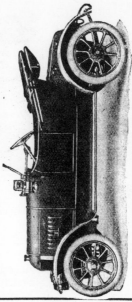
111

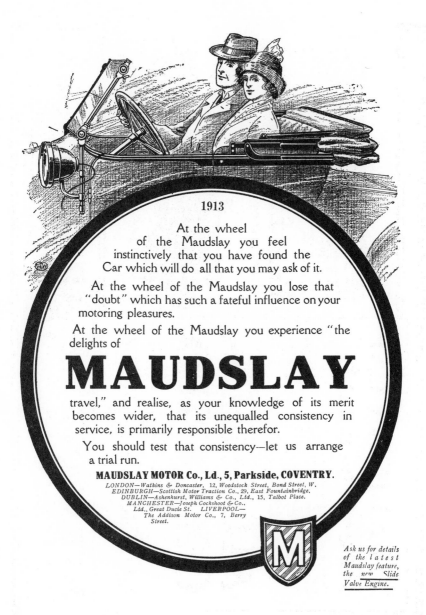

1913

At the wheel
of the Maudslay you feel
instinctively that you have found the
Car which will do all that you may ask of it.

At the wheel of the Maudslay you lose that "doubt" which has such a fateful influence on your motoring pleasures.

At the wheel of the Maudslay you experience "the delights of

MAUDSLAY

travel," and realise, as your knowledge of its merit becomes wider, that its unequalled consistency in service, is primarily responsible therefor.

You should test that consistency—let us arrange a trial run.

MAUDSLAY MOTOR Co., Ld., 5, Parkside, COVENTRY.
LONDON—Watkins & Doncaster, 12, Woodstock Street, Bond Street, W.
EDINBURGH—Scottish Motor Traction Co., 29, East Fountainbridge.
DUBLIN—Ashenhurst, Williams & Co., Ltd., 15, Talbot Place.
MANCHESTER—Joseph Cockshoot & Co.,
Ltd., Great Ducie St. LIVERPOOL—
The Addison Motor Co., 7, Berry
Street.

Ask us for details of the latest Maudslay feature, the new Slide Valve Engine.

Gentlemen—

1913

To any close observer of pneumatic tyre matters in general, the fact must strike forcibly home that Michelin ideas and Michelin designs are very consistently followed.

For this, there are the best of reasons: MICHELIN WAS THE FIRST TO DEVELOP AND APPLY THE PNEUMATIC TYRE TO THE REQUIREMENTS OF AUTOMOBILES; and, ever since that day, Michelin has been first in the field with every improvement effected in pneumatic tyre manufacture.

Thus, gentlemen, you can readily understand why it is that Michelin quality is the standard at which all tyre manufacturers aim. Michelin experience in the construction of car tyres is older, even as it is greater, than that of any other manufacturer. And it is a well-known fact that the Michelin manufacturing policy, right from the selection of raw material, through every stage of treatment, to the production of the finished article, is focussed upon a single objective: the production of one quality only—the best.

"Let us see what Michelin is doing" is a wall-text with tyre manufacturers.

THE MICHELIN TYRE CO., LTD., 81, FULHAM ROAD, LONDON, S.W.

No. 1 Bibendum Lectures.

114

'F.N.' CARS WIN DECISIVELY IN SOUTH AFRICA

1918

In the Annual Reliability Trial held by the South African Automobile Club, the first car home in the open class was an 11·9 F.N. with a petrol consumption of 36·54 ton miles and a total of 1,116 marks, the third place being taken by a 17·9 h.p. "F.N." (37·63 ton miles 1,013 marks.)

DELIVERY for EASTER.

"F.N." (England), Ltd.,

Showrooms—45-46, Clipstone St., London, W.
General Offices—106, Gt. Portland St., London, W. Repair Works — 31 and 32, Foley Street, Gt. Portland Street, Lond·n, W.

CAPE TOWN

C.D.C.

Four Models

11-16 H.P.
13-20 ,,
16-25 ,,
20-35 ,,
All 4 speeds.

1914

Agents—Write for Terms and Catalogue.

Fafnir, 211, Upper Thames Street,
LONDON, E.C.

1914

Vulcan

Britons! Never Despair!

His Majesty's Army Service Corps use Vulcan Cars.

Order <u>Your</u> Vulcan now and assist in keeping British workmen employed.

THE VULCAN MOTOR & ENGINEERING CO. (1906), Ltd.
SOUTHPORT.

THE VULCAN CAR AGENCY, Ltd., 166, Great Portland St., London, W.

Bradford Agents: The Jowett Motor Mfg. Co., Grosvenor Road, Bradford.

120

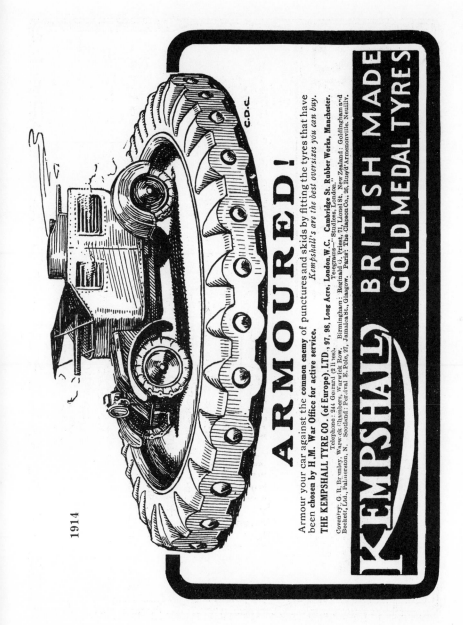

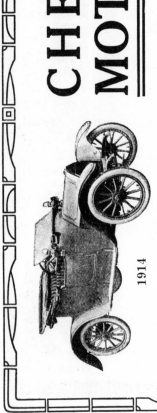

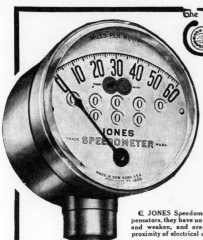

The JONES SPEEDOMETER

(And Gold Medal Turin Exhibition)

Latest Models for 1914—

with large bold figures, easily discernible :

with 3 in. dial, £4 4 0
with 4 in. dial, £5 5 0

The Jones is "Geared to the Truth," and cannot vary. Constructed on the principle of a natural law, unalterable and unvarying.

Every instrument individually calibrated by expert instrument makers.

❡ JONES Speedometers require no compensators, they have no magnets to depreciate and weaken, and are not affected by the proximity of electrical devices.

Markt & Co. (London) Ltd.,
98-100, Clerkenwell Road,
London, E.C.

1914

1   2   3

"Up and down in a jiffy"—
and the phrase is justified. for the

BEATONSON PATENT ONE-MAN HOOD

has really been designed for one-man handling, and is so constructed as to render its manipulation practically instantaneous. But its merit does not end there, and, as proof, note—

The perfectly straight bottom line—the absence of that lattice-work appearance so common among other hoods of similar design—the beautifully taut canvas stretch, and the clean, clear entrance back and front.

Note, and ask us for descriptive booklet—also particulars of the latest models of the

BEATONSON WIND SHIELD—

the shield with "the joint that differs" and makes adjustment simplicity itself.

G. Beaton & Son, Ltd., Dept. A, St. James's Sq., Notting Hill, London, W.

N.B.—Our latest line is the BEATONSON-TRIPLEX EXTENDING BACK SHIELD—it is adaptable to any small four-seater, and you can buy it for a £5 note.

NAPIER — THE PROVED BEST —

SIX-CYLINDER
MOTOR CARRIAGES

1917

THE ORIGINAL & LATEST
SIX-CYLINDER CAR
WHICH EMBODIES
Beauty, Refinement,
Silence,—and
Reliability.

PLEASE WRITE FOR PARTICULARS.

WORKS,
ACTON,
LONDON.W.

D·NAPIER & SON L^{TD}
14 New Burlington Street.
LONDON.W.

Strength

Austin 'TWENTY'

1919

"Life," "Sweetness," "Beauty"—essential though they be in a modern car, are of little account unless Strength also be present.

Austin "Twenty" strength is built-in strength. The safety factor is accurately calculated and allowed for, even in the smallest detail—because the "weakest link" determines the resistance of the whole.

THE AUSTIN MOTOR CO. LTD.

HEAD OFFICE - - - - NORTHFIELD, BIRMINGHAM

Telephone : King's Norton 230.   Telegrams : "Speedily, Northfield."

LONDON : 479-483 OXFORD ST., W.1.   AND AT PARIS

MANCHESTER : 130 DEANSGATE.   AND BRUSSELS

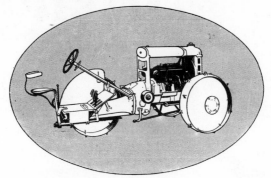

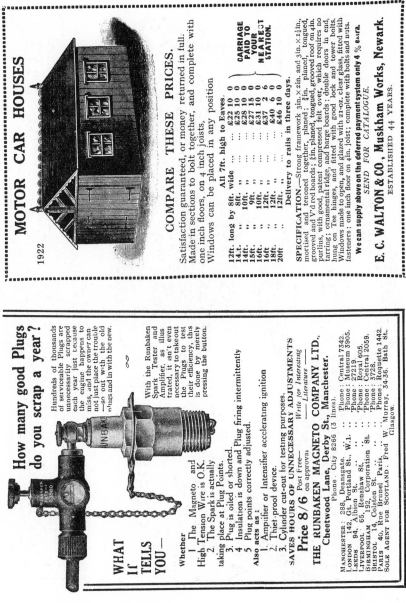

128

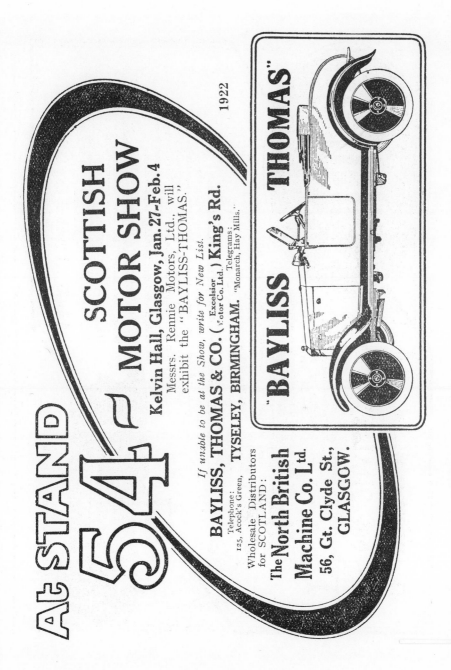
129

130

The 1922

CAR

£442

COMPLETE

THERE has never been a pause in the development of the CUBITT Car—where possible it has been refined and improved, and to-day—it is undoubtedly the finest value for money proposition on the market.

SHOULD any of our prospective customers care to avail themselves of our 'use it while you pay system' of £50 down, and the balance in monthly instalments, we should be pleased to forward full particulars on request.

"The Right Car at the Right Price."

BRIEF SPECIFICATION :

Engine : Four-cylinder 80 × 140 mm., four-speed, gate change, and reverse ; overhead worm-driven back axle ; wheelbase 10ft. 6in. ; road clearance 10½in. ; 815 × 105 Beldam Rubber Non-skid Tyres ; four-seater touring body, painted grey ; windscreen ; one-man hood ; five wheels ; four tyres ; electric lighting and starting set ; complete equipment of accessories

CUBITTS' ENGINEERING CO., LTD.

Showrooms   ..   ..   56, Conduit Street, London, W.
Service Station ..   ..   258, Gray's Inn Road, London, W.C.
Factory   ..   ..   Aylesbury, England.

J.C.F.

THE

1922 *Lanchester*

"FORTY"

The Epicyclic Change Speed Gear

THE accompanying illustration is of a complete set of Lanchester Epicyclic Change Speed Gears. A glance shows that they are totally unlike the gears on any other Car, and not only are they unlike in appearance, but in performance also. Silent changes are certain ; in fact, it is physically impossible to make a "noisy" change, and just as impossible to "miss" or "crash." The gears are always in mesh and are frictionally operated. No matter what the engine speed, any gear, including the reverse, may be immediately engaged with absolute certainty. The Lanchester Epicyclic Gear is unquestionably the simplest type yet produced. Will you allow us to demonstrate their efficiency to you in a trial run ?

We are exhibiting a 1922 model Lanchester "Forty" at Kelvin Hall, Glasgow, Jan. 27 to Feb. 4.

STAND No. 36

THE LANCHESTER MOTOR CO., LTD.,

95, New Bond Street,
London, W.

Armourer Mills,
Birmingham.

88, Deansgate,
Manchester.

Sole Agents for North & Central America, excluding Canada : Messrs. BREWSTER & Co., Inc., Long Island City, New York.

SCOTTISH SHOW
Kelvin Hall, GLASGOW
(Jan. 27th to Feb. 4th).

1922 "WOLSELEY"

The Cars which Combine Luxury with Economy

At the Scottish Motor Show, Glasgow, the world-famous Wolseleys will be on exhibition on the five stands enumerated below :

STAND No.

ROSSLEIGH, Ltd., Edinburgh - **28**

THOS. SHAW (Dundee), Ltd. - **29**

H. PROSSER, Glasgow - - **30**

A. C. PENMAN, Ltd., Dumfries **37**

CLAUD HAMILTON (Aberdeen) Ltd. **47**

The Wolseley range contains a Standard Model to meet EVERY Requirement.

The BRITISH-built ROVER Light CAR

RELIABLE. 1923 ECONOMICAL.

Cable from Edinburgh (Scotland), dated 12th May, 1923:

Scottish 6 Days' Trial, Six Rover 8's started, including one Coupe. Six finished, winning 3 Silver Cups and 3 Silver Medals. Every test hill was climbed by all six.

Cable from Coventry (England), dated 30th June, 1923:

Rover 8 Coupe, under R.A.C. observation, put up wonderful non-stop performance. 887 miles in 48 hours. Oil, 17; petrol, 47.60 miles per gallon.

8 H.P. TWO-SEATER ROVER.

SINGLE-SEATER, Australian Body .... £280 Nett

COMMERCIAL, Australian Body £280

DOUBLE SEATER, Australian Body £295

With Self Starter Fitted - £15 extra.

Easy Terms of Payment can be Arranged.

AUSTRALIAN DISTRIBUTORS:

N.S.W.: C. B. BRADLEY, LTD., 82 Bayswater Road, SYDNEY.
VICTORIA: LEVEY-COOPER MOTORS LTD., 124 a Beckett St., MELBOURNE.
QUEENSLAND: EVERS MOTOR CO., LTD., Adelaide Street, BRISBANE.

The Car that is different

1923

Hillman
The Guaranteed Car

Showing facia board, controls, pockets and screen wiper.

Method of storing side screens in felt lined locker.

Side screens on four seater adjusted as a V shaped rear screen.

Dicky seat opens with one revolving movement.

OPEN OR CLOSED CARRIAGE COMFORT
as occasion demands.

The patented Hillman rigid side screens form an all-weather equipment quite unique. When fully closed the Hillman All-weather Car has every appearance of a Saloon, and every comfort. When open touring conditions are preferred the Hillman has the advantage. *Whatever the weather the Hillman is right.* The 1924 Models have many added improvements both in chassis design and body comfort, and the coachwork is as always distinguished by its quality. At the reduced prices of £350 for the Two-Three Seater and £358 for the Four-Seater the 1924 Hillman represents remarkable value. The famous Hillman Twelve Months Guarantee remains the same.

Catalogues and agent's names from
The HILLMAN MOTOR CO. LTD.
COVENTRY

Hillman London Distributor:
143 149, Great Portland Street, W.1.

STAND NO.
101
OLYMPIA
NOV. 2 - 10

The Car that is different

The most outstanding Value ever offered by a British Motor Manufacturer!

1923

VULCAN

12 h.p. Four-Seater Car

IT seats four adults with comfort, climbs the steepest hill with ease and runs 30 miles on a gallon of petrol.

Owners appreciate its simplicity of control, excellent springing and graceful appearance. Behind every VULCAN is a 25 years' reputation.

The Equipment includes :

Real leather upholstery; Double folding windscreen; All-weather metal framed side curtains (adjustable to make rear-screen) ; One-man hood (black or brown); Adjustable driving seat; Electric lighting and starting; Clock; Speedometer; Bulb and electric horns; Luggage grid; Spring gaiters; Forced grease pump lubrication; Dunlop detachable wheels and tyres, including complete spare wheel and tyre; Detachable tool tray with full kit of tools; Licence holder; Number plates.
Finished—Blue, buff, grey, green, or maroon.

PRICE COMPLETE

£345

(At Works).

The Vulcan Motor & Engineering Co. (1906), Limited, SOUTHPORT.

LONDON — Vulcan Motors (London) Limited. 118, Great Portland Street, W.1.

Sales and Service Agents in every District.

See us at Olympia Stand 105

NEARLY 5,500 VULCANS MANUFACTURED AND SOLD SINCE AUGUST, 1919.

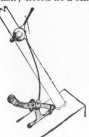
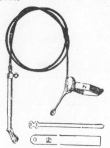

The Olympia Show

London Views the Greatest Automobile Exposition

Ever Held in the British Isles 1923

The 12–20 h. p. 4-cylinder Bianchi three-quarter coupe with body by Fountain, one of the many interesting models seen by London when they were displayed at the Olympia Show

By COUTTS BISS

THE Sixteenth International Motor Exposition held at Olympia and the White City, London, November 2nd to 11th, was international in the fullest sense of the word, and in consequence, of greater interest to the general public than the Paris Salon, which was confined largely to French cars. All of the newest designs of Continental European origin, displayed at the Salon, were shown at the London Exposition and, in addition, a much more representative collection of both American and British models.

Under royal patronage, the Show was favored with visits by the Prince of Wales and the Duke of York. The Prince, whose experience with Crossley cars was gained from the fleet of this make which accompanied him on his recent world tour, has purchased a new Crossley fitted with a magnificent

(Left) The interior of the new 40–50 h.p. 6-cylinder Napier with Cunard sedan-limousine body, showing its reversible auxiliary seats

sedan-limousine body, which was displayed on the Crossley stand, while his brother selected an Armstrong-Siddeley, fitted by the Connaught Motor & Carriage Company with a similar type of body.

A general survey of the trend of modern European automobile design, as reflected at the London Show, presents many interesting features, some of which appear to clash with popular opinion regarding detail of construction. Average figures taken

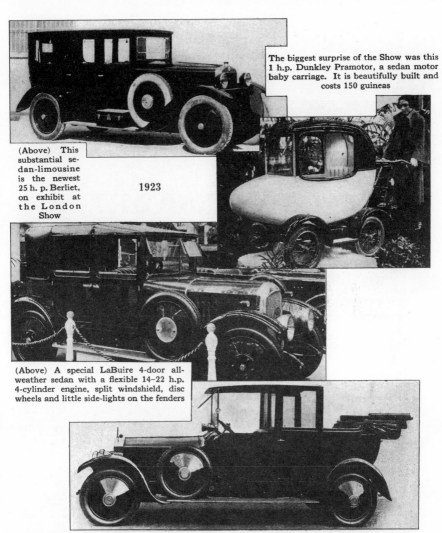

The biggest surprise of the Show was this 1 h.p. Dunkley Pramotor, a sedan motor baby carriage. It is beautifully built and costs 150 guineas

(Above) This substantial sedan-limousine is the newest 25 h. p. Berliet, on exhibit at the London Show

1923

(Above) A special LaBuire 4-door all-weather sedan with a flexible 14–22 h.p. 4-cylinder engine, split windshield, disc wheels and little side-lights on the fenders

from the models exhibited give a very accurate idea of the question of motor style exactly as it stands to-day on this side of the ocean.

One of the most gorgeous cars at Olympia was this 40–50 h.p. Rolls Royce limousine-landaulet (above) with body made by Hooper for the Marquis of Londonderry. It is extremely conservative, with dark blue finish

The 4-cylinder engine holds a marked preponderance over all rivals, in spite of the introduction of several small and medium size 6-cylinder engines on the one hand and small 2-cylinder engines, both air and water cooled, on the other. Four-cylinder engines represented three-quarters of the models shown and of this large number it is interesting to note that one-fifth were rated at less than 10 h.p., one-fifth at over 16 h.p., while the remaining three-fifths ranged between 10 and 16 h.p., by the British Treasury rating which admittedly only takes into calculation the bore of the engine. It is perhaps a better indication of the general requirements of the British market when, upon analysis, it is found that more than half of the 4-cylinder engines exhibited were under 12 h.p.

The Paris Salon 1923

The Largest Automobile Show Ever Held in France Emphasizes Smaller Cars and Higher Prices with Increased Use of Four Wheel Brakes

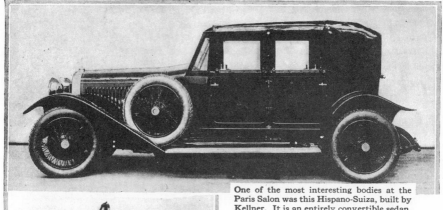

One of the most interesting bodies at the Paris Salon was this Hispano-Suiza, built by Kellner. It is an entirely convertible sedan. Beautiful workmanship distinguishes its top and its disappearing pillars and windows

The posts separating the two side doors fold over onto the back of the driver's seat, when the car is open, as in the lower picture. This stunning car is trimmed with a gray-green cloth with inlaid gray maple fittings

By COUTTS BISS

THE Seventeenth French Automobile Exhibition drew so large a number of applications that the Grand Palais was not of sufficient size to hold them all and it was necessary to stage the trucks, delivery cars, small cars, motorcycles and stationary engines in two other buildings across the river; an arrangement which proved convenient except, perhaps, to those manufacturers who were showing small cars in addition to their larger models. In these instances, visitors were unable to see the full range of their models grouped together on one stand.

The Paris Salon has not the same international atmosphere as the London Show. For instance, the American exhibit included only

Cadillac, Chevrolet, Buick, Oakland, Oldsmobile and Overland. Of foreign countries, perhaps Italy was best represented, and then Belgium. Great Britain had only a poor representation, by comparison, and ex-enemy countries were excluded entirely.

The appearance of the Salon was much improved by the elimination of the standards bearing the name-boards of the various firms over their exhibits. These boards were slung, instead, from the balcony across the hall, with the exception of the central dome, which, owing to its height, did not admit of this arrangement. The colour scheme, in blue and cream, was very pleasing and carried out with characteristic French taste.

The most interesting feature of the exhibition to hardened visitors was, naturally, the number of entirely new models which were staged apart from previous models of the same companies. Ballot showed his new 4-cylinder models. Bugatti appeared with two new 8-

The cabriolet above, on an 18 h. p. Peugeot chassis, is entirely collapsible and, in its open position, looks exactly like a large touring car. It is beautifully fitted, has extra seats facing forward, with very comfortable adjustable backs, and is toned in gray, both inside and out

The Voisin car is attracting considerable attention in France just now, as one of Europe's best mass-production automobiles. Above is shown a new cabriolet displayed at the Paris Salon by its builders, Million-Guiet

Above is shown one of the custom built Farman cars at the Paris Salon. This is a cabriolet by Kellner, fully collapsible, with wooden artillery wheels and a blue finish throughout, with lemon wood inlaid work

cylinder, cars, while De Dion Bouton revealed three brand new models. Delaunay-Belleville, Hotchkiss, Itala and Unic, each presented a new small model, while Peugeot introduced five new cars, including one with a valveless engine on the Knight principle.

The tendency of the Show was a still further increase in engine capacity with greatly decreased engine size compared with previous years. And this statement is made without taking into consideration the small cars and cyclecars displayed in the temporary buildings. There were, of course, many fast and powerful vehicles in the 6-cylinder class including Renault, Farman, Hispano-Suiza and Rolls-Royce; among the 8-cylinder cars, Panhard and Isotta-Fraschini; and, in a class by itself, the big new 12-cylinder Fiat, the only 12-cylinder automobile in the exposition.

Four-cylinder engines were still in the majority although there was a discernible endeavor to exploit the 6-cylinder machines of much smaller dimensions than has been customary heretofore. All of the better known makes are producing small, and in some cases diminutive, models, an example of which is the little 6 h. p. Renault.

At the Paris Salon there were some half dozen examples of the 2-cylinder engine, consigned to the smallest class and, except in the case of the Morgan, which is, of course, well known in England, used only in cars unknown outside of the country of their origin.

Air-cooling is making very little progress over here in Europe. At the Salon this principle was found only in a few of the smallest models and water-

cooling by pump was used in a slightly larger number of cars than the natural thermo-syphon system. There is a marked increase in the number of makers utilizing overhead valves. They have been adopted by De Dion for the first time. Bianchi uses them on his new Italian models, as do Delage on the new 6-cylinder model and Fiat in its new Super Six. Peugeot introduced various models, some with overhead valves, some with valves side by side and others without valves, that is to say, with the Knight engine with its sleeve action. The Bignan company, after lengthy tests on their racing cars, introduced at the Salon a positive valve-closing mechanism, by which the use of springs is eliminated, driven by an overhead camshaft running in a bath of oil. They claim that this gear has proved itself efficient on an engine running up to 5000 r.p.m.

Aluminum pistons were shown in the majority of engines, but at least two makers, Voisin and Bignan, employed magnesium pistons, which are very expensive at present, owing to difficulties of casting; but when these are overcome the magnesium piston has advantages which will entail its more frequent use.

The magneto still holds its own and in the few cases where battery ignition was fitted, it was generally the Delco. It is interesting to note here that the new 20 H.P. 6-cylinder Rolls-Royce, which has just made its bow to the public, is fitted with battery ignition. This car was not shown at the Paris Salon but a demonstration car was very busy on the streets of Paris in the neighborhood of the Show.

1923

Some of the town car bodies on Renault cars were well worth inspection. One of them is shown at the left, a majestic limousine by Million-Guiet with every conceivable motoring comfort and lines which spell power and speed

In the Rolls-Royce stand was this landaulet painted blue and trimmed with gray, with auxiliary seats disappearing into elaborate inlaid cabinets

The preponderance of spiral bevel gears in rear axle construction was most noticeable. The spiral bevel was fitted in more than double the number of models using the straight bevel, while the worm gear, apparently, is almost extinct, the only firms of importance using it being Peugeot and Talbot-Darracq, but neither firm utilizing the worm gear on all its models. Unit construction of engine and gear box with the gear and brake lever mounted on top of the gear box revealed an increasing number of adherents and doubtless will soon be the recognized system of the majority of manufacturers, since this design has so many marked advantages which certainly outweigh its disadvantages. It may be noted here again that this is the practice followed in the new Rolls-Royce.

An increase in the use of four-wheel brakes was naturally looked for, but this increase was, perhaps, greater than was expected. Among the firms exploiting this growing form of braking were Ballot, Berliet, Bugatti, De Dion Bouton, Farman, Fiat, Lancia, Peugeot, Renault and Talbot-Darracq. In most cases, however, front wheel brakes were not fitted to all the models exhibited by these firms, although it would appear to be only a question of a short time before this highly desirable feature is incorporated in all up-to-date automobiles. The front wheel brakes were not restricted to the powerful models only, for they were found on the Voisin 8 h. p., the Bignan 12 h. p. the Delage 11 h. p. and the Leon Bollee 12 h. p. They are fitted also in the new light Lancia, which was, perhaps, from a constructional point of view, the most interesting car in the Show, and which was described superficially in this magazine last month.

The three main types of front wheel brakes are the Perrot, the Isotta-Fraschini and the Adex, most of which are used by various car makers on a royalty basis, but Bugatti and Unic use special front wheel braking systems of their own.

The straight sided tire has made no headway, aside from its use in racing cars, on which this type is more generally employed. It showed no advance at the Salon.

As to body work at the Salon, there is not a great deal to be said. To my mind, the Renaults were the most interesting, because they were shown in a number of smart town car models which were highly artistic, although conservative. The photographs accompanying this article give an idea of the beautiful bodies exhibited at the Salon.

THE WONDER CAR OF 1930

THE SENSATIONAL NEW HILLMAN STRAIGHT EIGHT SALOON AT £445

1930

Up–to–date in every respect—Thermostatically controlled Radiator Shutters, Chromium Plating, Marles Steering, etc. Exceptional smoothness and flexibility, wonderfully fine suspension, greater acceleration—these are some of the many outstanding features of the new Hillman " Straight Eight " — the lowest priced British " Straight Eight " and the pioneer of inexpensive eight cylinder motoring.

Write to–day for our Catalogue H/35 and copy of The Hon. Mrs. Victor Bruce's book, " From Arctic to Mediterranean in 91 hours."

STRAIGHT EIGHT

Tourer	£430
Safety Tourer	£445
Saloon	£445
Safety Saloon	£485
*6-Light Weymann Saloon	£485
*Segrave Model	£495
Drop-Head Coupé	£510

FOURTEEN

Tourer	£310
Safety Tourer	£325
Saloon	£325
Safety Saloon	£375
*6-Light Weymann Saloon	£375
*Segrave Model	£385
Drop-Head Coupé	£415

*Sunshine Roof £10 extra.
Triplex glass on Safety Models.
Dunlop tyres standard.

THE HILLMAN MOTOR CAR CO. LTD.
COVENTRY.

World Exporters: Rootes Ltd.,
Devonshire House, Piccadilly, W.1.

1932

ROLLS-ROYCE
The Best Car in the World

ROLLS-ROYCE LTD. 14-15 CONDUIT STREET, LONDON. W.I.

ENDURING QUALITY...

LOOK UNDERNEATH THE CAR YOU BUY

No car may be judged from superficial appearance alone. Graceful lines and a pretty body are valueless unless based upon a chassis designed from every point of view to stand up to hard service.

This is doubly true where cars of unusually high performance are concerned. Glance at these views of the Renault "Speed Six," a car in which robustness and performance have been made twin ideals of its famous manufacturers.

For £285 you may now take the wheel of a 70 m.p.h. car and do your economical 20 m.p.g. with the assurance that you at last drive a car that will never "wear out."

RENAULT

1932

RENAULT "SPEED SIX" £285

RENAULT "TEN "	- - £210	"BIG FOUR"	- - -	£275
SPEED "FOUR"	- - £215	"BIG SIX"	- - -	£380
	28 H.P. "STRAIGHT EIGHT" £515			

For details and trial run write or 'phone to:

RENAULT LTD.
21 PALL MALL, LONDON, S.W.1 (Phone: Whitehall 7270)

Make Yours a

CITROËN for 1932! The finest range of 4-cylinder and 6-cylinder cars ever produced from the Citroën Works at Slough, Buckinghamshire, where none but British labour is employed and to which famous British firms supply materials. New 1932 features include Rear Petrol Tank, "Starter" Carburettor, Improved Engine, Improved Road Performance, Lower and Wider Bodies, more Luxurious Interiors, Dipping Headlamp Reflectors, Wire or Disc Wheels, Spare Wheel at Side, Window Ventilating Louvres and Glass Sun Visor, etc., on De-Luxe Models. 4-cylinder Models from **£195**. 6-cylinder Models from **£295.**

Send To-Day for a Copy of New " Somewhere In Britain " Folder No. 17.

CITROËN CARS LIMITED
Citroën Building, Brook Green
Hammersmith, London, W.6
Telephone : Riverside 2220/6

West End Showrooms : Devonshire House
Piccadilly, London, W.1   Mayfair 5403

Prices from :
£195

"Big 12" De-Luxe Saloon - - **£225**

Products of Citroën Works, Slough, Buckinghamshire

The Humber "16/50" Six-light Saloon

★ Every third HUMBER owner you meet was a motorist before the war

1932

At least 18 years' accumulated experience guided these men in making their choice

★ *The figures quoted in this advertisement are the result of an investigation recently carried out among 5,000 modern Humber owners. It also showed that 87.5% of the new Humbers are the choice of men who have owned at least six cars before.*

HUMBER

"16/50" from £395.   "SNIPE" from £435.   "PULLMAN" from £735.
Triplex glass throughout.   Prices ex factory.   Special scheme of extended payments.

Humber Ltd., Coventry.   London Service Depot: Canterbury Road Kilburn. N.W.6.   London Show-rooms & Export Dept.: Rootes Ltd., Devonshire House, London W.1.

AS . DEPENDABLE . AS . AN . AUSTIN

1 in 4 *"Enthusiastic about the Seven? I should say I am!—and I'm not the only one . . . for the registration figures show that every FOURTH new car sold in Great Britain during the last trading year ending July 31, 1931, was an Austin!"*

THE AUSTIN SEVEN DE LUXE SALOON (On Long Wheelbase)

Your pocket will tell you *why* it's the most popular light car!

What is the reason for the obvious and overwhelming popularity of the Austin Seven . . . why do more motorists choose this light car than any other ? Ask an owner—and he will tell you that you will never fully realise why *until you run an Austin Seven . . . until* you see for yourself how supremely well it combines the joys of motoring with the even more important needs of the pocket.

The six inches increase in wheelbase on the latest model, and the greater comfort and ease of riding it affords . . . the finer appearance and better finish . . .

the new headlamps with a dipping beam device . . . all these are features that contribute to the pleasure of motoring. And they are features whose worth you can prove by actual inspection and trial.

But you can have little conception of the amazingly low running costs, the unfailing dependability of this giant-hearted light car until after months of day in, day out service. Run an Austin Seven, and then you will know—for your pocket will tell you—why it is the most popular of all light cars.

THE SEVEN DE LUXE SALOON *on long wheelbase, as illustrated* Standard Saloon on long wheelbase £118; Tourer or Two-Seater on short wheelbase £118. Prices at works. Chromium finish, Triplex glass throughout and Dunlop tyres standard. **£128**

READ THE AUSTIN MAGAZINE: 4d. EVERY MONTH

1932 **AUSTIN 7**

 The Austin Motor Company Limited, Longbridge, Birmingham. Showrooms, also Service Station for the Austin Seven: 479-483 Oxford Street, London, W.1. Showrooms and Service Station: Holland Park Hall, W.11.

150

MD1932

a car that

looks the part . . .

1932

this self-assured OXFORD

The Morris range also includes the MINOR (from £100), FAMILY EIGHT (from £152 10s.), COWLEY (from £165), MAJOR '6' (from £199 10s.) and the ISIS '6' (£350). *All Prices ex Works.*

MORRIS FIT TRIPLEX GLASS THROUGHOUT

Send a postcard to ENQUIRIES DEPT., COWLEY, for illustrated catalogue; full details of service facilities, name of your nearest dealer to whom to apply for free trial run, and if required how to purchase out of income.

MORRIS MOTOR HOUSES

Strong, fire-resisting. Steel or wood frame, asbestos panels, roll-aside doors. Easy to erect. Prices from £9 15s.

MORRIS MOTORS LIMITED
COWLEY - - OXFORD

Service Advertising MO6c

"Don't judge by appearances" they say. Yet in the Oxford there is no truer guide to its mechanical perfection than the fine finish and shapely lines. And the Oxford is so versatile. It murmurs through traffic, held in instant check by its noiseless Lockheed hydraulic brakes; sets the pace on the open road, taking the long tiresome hills on the 'silent third' of its twin-top 4-speed gearbox. Such is the excellent and economical Oxford—a car to be proud of in any company.

4-DOOR SALOON *(with Pytchley flush-type sliding head)*	- -	**£265**
2-DOOR 4-SEATER COUPE *(with Pytchley flush-type sliding head)*	-	**£275**
2-DOOR 4-SEATER SPORTS COUPE		**£285**
(with Pytchley flush-type sliding head)		*ex Works.*

BRIEF SPECIFICATION: 6-cyl. 14.9 h.p. (tax £15). S.U. carburation with special air pre-heater and cleaner, which consumes all crankcase fumes. All-straight frame, long semi-elliptic gaitered springing, double acting shock absorbers. Lucas lighting, starting and coil ignition. Finger-tip controls, including headlight dipper on steering column, 5 Magna type wire wheels, Dunlop tyres, chromium finish. 'Eddyfree' front. Leather upholstery. Backed by Morris Universal Service.

MORRIS CARS ARE GUARANTEED FOR 2 YEARS

MORRIS OXFORD '6'

¹⁹³³ # Never Beaten!

72 hours continuous running, at an average speed of 38·5 m.p.h.

Further, the Jowett "Kestrel" was towing a trailer weighing 14 cwts. and throughout the whole of the 72 hours terrific pounding, not one moment's trouble was experienced. Now, what about the "little engine with the big pull"?

The Hon. Victor and Mrs. Bruce, who drove the car, send us their congratulations on making such a car.

We, in return, congratulate them.

You may have a Montlhery Jowett exactly as Mr. Bruce for his Jowett is absolutely standard.

Prices from £135.   Tax £7.

JOWETT CARS LTD., IDLE, BRADFORD

(Observed by Auto Club de France).

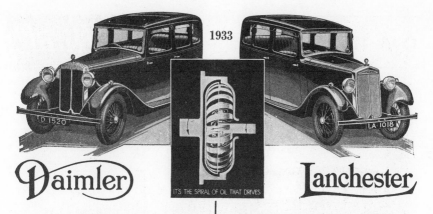

1933

Daimler

IT'S THE SPIRAL OF OIL THAT DRIVES

Lanchester

"I would like to take this opportunity to say how pleased I am with the performance of the 15 h.p. Daimler. I have been used to high power American cars and expected a lot of gear changing on hills. But in practice I find the Daimler takes the hills in a wonderful way, and when gear has to be changed the fluid flywheel has made a pleasure of it. In many other ways I think you have the finest car of its class on the road, and I am sure it will have a very big sale."—R.E.W.

"I am more than pleased with the two Daimler Cars ('20' and '25') delivered to me recently. They are a great advance on anything I have experienced in 22 years' driving. The transmission system is all that you claim for it, the delightful smoothness is a real joy to myself and an eye opener to those of my friends trying it for the first time."—C.J.T.

"The Lanchester '10' which I bought from you before Xmas is by far the most satisfactory car I have owned since 1913, and I have had many since I started motoring in 1911 and in several parts of the world.

I had no idea the chassis was so well thought out, and so well finished. The fluid flywheel is uncanny and makes the gearbox twice as attractive and fascinating to use.

The run from London here is 247 miles, and I was not a bit tired at the end of it, which I usually am. The body is also really good and the steering, brakes and springing splendid. Except for the car mentioned in 1913, I have always been more or less disappointed in any of the many cars I have bought since. It is therefore a great pleasure to let you know what a pleasant surprise this Lanchester is. I cannot find fault with it and it continues to 'grow on' one."—W.H.B.

DAIMLER FLUID FLYWHEEL TRANSMISSION

must be tried to be appreciated fully. Ask for a demonstration run at once—there are authorized Dealers everywhere. We will gladly send you full details of the cars if you will mark with a cross the model most likely to interest you, put your name and address in the space below and post to THE DAIMLER CO., LTD. 71 Sandy Lane, COVENTRY.

DAIMLER '15' - £450.   '20' - £725.   '25' - £950.   '40' - £1,550.   '50' - £1,650.
LANCHESTER '10' - £315.   '18' - £595.   Triplex Glass throughout.

THE EASIEST CARS IN THE WORLD TO CONTROL

DAIMLER *Fluid*

1933

DAIMLER

All Daimler models are fitted with Daimler Fluid Flywheel Transmission

DAIMLER
'15' Saloon
from **£450**

DAIMLER
'15' Sports Saloon
£465

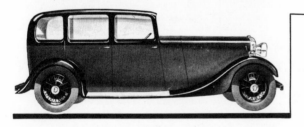

DAIMLER
'20' Saloon
from **£695**

AT OLYMPIA STAND No. 138

Ask a Daimler, Lanchester or B.S.A. Dealer for a

DAIMLER *Fluid Flywheel* TRANSMISSION

1933

B. S. A.

All B.S.A. "10" models are fitted with Daimler Fluid Flywheel Transmission

B. S. A.
Varsity Saloon

£275

B. S. A.
Saloon

from **£230**

B. S. A.
Peerless Coupe

£268

AT OLYMPIA STAND No. 115

THE DAIMLER CO. LTD., 70 SANDY LANE, COVENTRY

ARMSTRONG SIDDELEY
Pioneers of "Better" Motoring

The modern Armstrong Siddeley has made motoring so pleasant, safe and reliable that it is hard to imagine any further improvement.

Armstrong Siddeley pioneered the pre-selective self-changing gear, proved leader in perfect control ; four wheel jacks, another owner-driver feature successfully foreseen and fitted; central chassis lubrication ; stylish coachwork with ample room; saloon ventilation without draught; the ideal solution of the luggage carrying problem ; springing that is supple yet stable at speed; and durability to withstand long sustained use.

1933

**ARMSTRONG SIDDELEY
MOTORS LIMITED
COVENTRY, ENGLAND**

London : 10 Old Bond Street, W.1
Manchester : 35 King Street West

1933

TEN

'Torquay' Saloon

with

Self-Changing Box

£325

THE CROSSLEY 'TORQUAY'
10 H.P. SALOON

CR 60

Other 10 h.p. models:

'BUXTON' SALOON WITH SELF-CHANGING BOX - - - - -	£298
'BUXTON' SALOON WITH SILENT THIRD - - - - -	£278
'TORQUAY' SALOON WITH SILENT THIRD - - - - -	£305

IF you have not tried the Crossley Ten make sure you do so before deciding on your next car. Among the special features of the Crossley Ten are: ROOMINESS—the wheelbase is over 9 ft., an important feature which you should take into account before committing yourself to a smaller car. ROADHOLDING—The roadholding qualities of the Crossley Ten must be experienced to be believed, they are phenomenal. SILENCE—The peculiar silence of the Crossley Ten is due to scientific design and superb engineering skill. The bodies are a triumph of craftsmanship, the 'Torquay' body, incidentally, was the champion light car in the Coachwork Competition of the 1932 R.A.C. RALLY.

Larger Crossley Models:

SILVER CROSSLEY SALOON (15.6 h.p.)	£495
GOLDEN CROSSLEY SALOON (20.9 h.p.)	£575
ENCLOSED LIMOUSINE (7-str.)	£875
ENC. LANDAULETTE (7-seater)	£895

Crossley Motors Limited, Gorton, Manchester, or 50 Page Street, Westminster, London, S.W.1

HERE'S EVIDENCE · ·

The 1935 Standards are advanced up-to-date editions of the Standard cars which were so overwhelmingly successful in 1934.

EXPERTS TESTED THEM AND FOUND THEM *GOOD!*

1935

READ THESE :—

"*The Standard Ten de Luxe Saloon is attractive outside, inside, in performance, in control and in price.*"

THE TIMES

"*The performance (of the Standard "Twelve") is equal to that of many sports cars of the same capacity.*"

THE SCOTSMAN

"*Big-car performance with small-car economy.*"

THE AUTOCAR

"*A thoroughly practical medium-sized car, bearing the stamp of good workmanship, and experienced design, which is excellent value.*"

THE MOTOR

OF THE EXCELLENCE OF

OWNERS WHOLEHEARTEDLY PRAISED THEM

READ THESE :—

"*I could never wish to be served more faithfully by any car.*"

M. J. Hants.

"*I have nothing for it (the 10 h.p. Standard) but the highest praise.*"

W.A.P. Bude

"*Congratulations on a very fine job, and the best of luck for 1935.*"

S.E.W. London

(*The original letters from which the above extracts are quoted can be seen in the offices of the Standard Motor Co. Ltd., Canley, Coventry*).

"*I should like to express to you my appreciation of the wonderful service this car has given me.*"

F.H.S. London

THE 1935 STANDARD RANGE

PRICES: (*Ex works*) "Nine" (*two-door*) £145, £155. (*Four-door*) £165, £175. "Ten" £185 to £245. "Twelve" £215 to £255 (*Radio Model*). "Sixteen" £285. "Twenty" £395. New "Speed 10-12" models £245 to £295.

Triplex Glass   Dunlop Tyres

Write for 1935 literature to :—

THE STANDARD MOTOR CO. LTD.,
CANLEY, COVENTRY.

'Phone : Coventry 3181. Telegrams: "Flywheel Coventry". West End Showrooms : "Standard Cars" 37 Davies Street, Grosvenor Square, London, W.1. 'Phone : Mayfair 5011.

THE 1935 STANDARDS

The product of

70 years' experience

in precision engineering

BSA 1934

MADE UNDER THE TECHNICAL SUPERVISION OF THE DAIMLER CO. LTD.

Some B.S.A. Features

1 Pre-selective self-changing Gearbox.

2 Cruciform-braced frame.

3 Engine flexibly mounted at five points.

4 Absence of gear lever gives extra room in front and greatly increases driving comfort.

1934

B.S.A. "10" SALOON

with Daimler Fluid Flywheel Transmission

from **£230**

B.S.A. CARS LTD., 113, SANDY LANE, COVENTRY

1934

"THE FASTEST 1,100 c.c. CAR IN THE WORLD"

says "The Motor" (30/10/34) when speaking of the "Truly Magic Magnette" . . . the MG car that has just collected a further bag of records at speeds of up to 128·70 m.p.h.

¶ During the past few years the really enormous number of successes attained by MG cars testifies . . . beyond dispute . . . to their consistency . . . to their sturdiness . . . to their reliability. Spectacular successes are impressive — but success following upon success with inexorable regularity justifies the makers' claim that the MG is the Best Small Car in the World.

★ *Full range of the latest* MG *cars in our showrooms* ★

Sole London MG Distributors

"THE CAR THAT HAS MADE WINNING A HABIT."

UNIVERSITY MOTORS LIMITED

Established a Quarter of a Century

STRATTON HOUSE - - PICCADILLY, W.1

GROSVENOR 4141 (14 lines)

EROS

THE ROVER PROGRAMME FOR 1935

Proved Quality
Proved Reliability
Proved Features

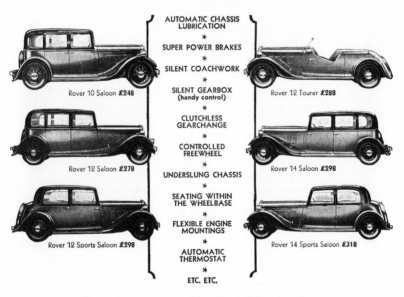

AUTOMATIC CHASSIS
LUBRICATION
*
SUPER POWER BRAKES
*
SILENT COACHWORK
*
SILENT GEARBOX
(handy control)
*
CLUTCHLESS
GEARCHANGE
*
CONTROLLED
FREEWHEEL
*
UNDERSLUNG CHASSIS
*
SEATING WITHIN
THE WHEELBASE
*
FLEXIBLE ENGINE
MOUNTINGS
*
AUTOMATIC
THERMOSTAT
*
ETC. ETC.

Rover 10 Saloon £248

Rover 12 Saloon £278

Rover 12 Sports Saloon £298

Rover 12 Tourer £288

Rover 14 Saloon £298

Rover 14 Sports Saloon £318

The new Rover programme, some examples of which are shown above, continues the outstanding refinement of the 1934 models and combines this important quality with a further improved performance. *Full illustrated catalogue will gladly be sent upon request to*

THE ROVER CO. LTD., COVENTRY

London Showrooms: Henly's Ltd., Devonshire House, Piccadilly, W.1
London Service Depot: Seagrave Road, Fulham

CVS—123

1935

George Eyston

says

THE S.S. HAS "SPARKLING PERFORMANCE"

★

Mr. G. E. T. EYSTON
the famous racing motorist who holds
more International Class records than
any other British Racing Driver.

"I am very pleased with the 20 h.p. S.S. It not only has a sparkling performance which includes excellent steering and braking, but the characteristic smartness of its external appearance is by no means superficial. All details of the coachwork and chassis have been carefully planned by a practical designer, which is worthy of the highest praise. The comfort and ease of handling under all conditions is a delight." (Signed) George Eyston. Like many other motoring experts,

Mr. George Eyston is enthusiastic about the performance of the S.S. You, too, will be delighted when you try it for yourself. Arrange for a trial run now or write for art catalogue.

S.S.I. prices, 20 h.p. models, £340 to £365. 16 h.p., £335 to £360. S.S.II. prices, 12 h.p. models, £265 to £270. 10 h.p., £260 to £265.

S.S. CARS LTD., HOLBROOK LANE, COVENTRY

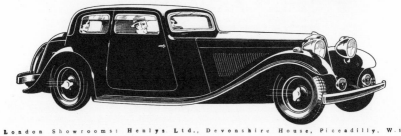

London Showrooms: Henlys Ltd., Devonshire House, Piccadilly, W.1

1935 # RAILTON

"Ten years ahead of its time"
(THE AUTOCAR)

THE CAR WITH THE
BEST PERFORMANCE

can be seen on the following Stands at Olympia Motor Show

Nos. 1 — 3 — 8 — 40A and 89

Chassis £433   Complete Cars from £553

RAILTON CARS, FAIRMILE, COBHAM, SURREY.   Phone: COBham 400.

RENAULT AIRLINE

Air currents not only concern the pilot but the motorist. That is why the designers of the Renault 'Airline' make good use of the knowledge and experience of the leading aircraft designers of the day. The Renault 'Airline' is styled for the city streets, streamlined for the open road, sprung for the roughest byway. Its engine is a miracle of strength combined with lightness, and all the well-known Renault features, such as transverse rear springing, synchro gears, flexible engine mountings, easy fit jacking, built-in luggage and spare wheel housings, are included in its specification.

1935

12 H.P. Airline Saloon £198
(with sliding roof £207 . 10s.)
13·9 H.P. Airline Saloon £220
(including sliding roof.)

Write for illustrated folder to :

RENAULT LTD. SEAGRAVE ROAD, WEST BROMPTON, LONDON, S.W.6 (Fulham 3301)
West End Showrooms : 21 PALL MALL, LONDON, W.1 (Whitehall 7270)

The only car that could possibly take the place of the old Riley "9" has taken 8 years to build!

1935

HERE'S the NEW RILEY "NINE"

WHAT a wealth of experience has been built into this car! With what a pedigree, a reputation, does it start life! For a twelvemonth the motor trade hummed with rumours of it. Experienced motor traders ordered it before it had been assembled!

Now it is here, for you to see and drive. Entirely re-designed and re-priced to appeal to a new and wider market. Aeroline body, all-steel, of amazing strength—inter-axle seating, without which perfect passenger comfort is unattainable—clear front floor, so that the driver need not step out of the offside door into a traffic stream—Pre-selectagear, uncrashable, easiest of all gear-change systems and incidentally the most costly to manufacture—capacious luggage locker under cover—easy jacking, automatic chassis lubrication, concealed direction indicators, chromium bumpers—every worth-while accessory and trouble-saving device. Visit the local Riley Showrooms today.

In 1933/4 the Riley Nine with Pre-selectagear Transmission cost £325. Today you can own this NEW Riley Nine for ——

£269

TAX £6-15-0

The new Nine is one of the finest, widest range of cars the Riley Company has ever built. Other models include the 1½ Litre, the 15 h.p. Six and an entirely new model, the Eight-Ninety (appearing at Olympia). Prices from £269 to £450. Dunlop Tyres and Triplex Glass.

RILEY (COVENTRY) LIMITED, COVENTRY

THE MOST SUCCESSFUL CAR IN THE WORLD

Riley

Austin ARROW

1935 COACHWORK ON AUSTIN SPECIAL SPORTS CHASSIS

£274

AUSTIN TEN
Special
Sports Chassis
ARROW
Sports 2-Seater

AUSTIN TEN
Special
Sports Chassis
ARROW
Full 4-Seater

£274

£207

AUSTIN SEVEN
Special
"75" Sports Chassis
ARROW
Competition 2-Seater

AUSTIN SEVEN
Special
"65" Sports Chassis
ARROW
Sports 2-Seater

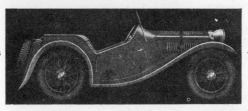

£189

H.A.SAUNDERS
THE AUSTIN DISTRIBUTORS & SOLE PROPRIETORS
AUSTIN ARROW COACHWORK
'Phone:
SPEEDWELL
5061-2-3
140-144, GOLDERS GREEN Rd. GOLDERS GREEN, LONDON N.W.11

A little more cost...

1935

...a lot more style

"Style," as possessed by Standard cars and described by the dictionary is "*noticeably superior quality*." It is the result of a method of design and manufacture which is not " bullied " by questions of price. That is why you pay a little more for a Standard. It is also the reason why Standard cars are "cheapest in the long run." Because careful British workmanship and finest materials yield dividends — in long life and faithful service.

Write for 1935 literature to :—THE STANDARD MOTOR CO., LTD., CANLEY, COVENTRY

MODELS
from 9 h.p. to 20 h.p.
PRICES (*ex works*)
from £145 to £450
Dunlop Tyres. Triplex Glass

West End Showrooms :
" Standard Cars,"
37, Davies Street,
Grosvenor Square,
London, W.1.

THE CAR IT PAYS TO PAY A LITTLE MORE FOR

GAFFIKIN WILKINSON
for

LAGONDA

1936

PRICES :

CHASSIS - **£795**
TOURER - **£1,000**
SALOON - **£1,085**

AN unbroken connection with LAGONDA extending over 9 years enables us to state authoritatively that the new 1936 4½ litre Models, developed and perfected by Mr. W. O. Bentley, are the finest examples of this high calibre British car as yet produced.

As officially appointed Retailers for LAGONDA we offer the earliest deliveries.

These cars can be seen and inspected during the Show at 28, Berkeley Street, where one of our representatives will be in attendance. Trial runs can be arranged at 17a, Hanover Square.

We hold the largest stock of reconditioned Lagonda Cars.

GAFFIKIN WILKINSON
& CO., LTD.

17a, HANOVER SQUARE, LONDON, W.1.

Telephone : MAYFAIR 5335.

SHOWROOMS & SERVICE DEPOT AT THE SAME ADDRESS

1935

The Seventeen or Twenty h.p. Coachbuilt Saloon, cars of dignity and distinction, £465 and £550 respectively.

Armstrong Siddeley will have the finest range of quality cars at Olympia

WITH their exclusive styles of coachwork the Armstrong Siddeley series of fine cars will be the most distinguished cars at Olympia. They appeal by reason of their very quality and good taste. They offer that comfort and luxury found only in a carriage-built body. They are superbly finished and are remarkable for the way they retain their exceptional performance, endurance, and attractive appearance.

See and try the new Twelve-Plus

(14 H.P. R.A.C. Rating)

ARMSTRONG
SIDDELEY

With the only proved self changing gear

Twelve - *from £275*
Twelve - Plus *from £295*
Seventeen *from £385*
Twenty - *from £550*
and the Siddeley Special

Please write for Catalogue "A.162"

ARMSTRONG SIDDELEY MOTORS LTD., COVENTRY
LONDON: 10 OLD BOND STREET, W.1   MANCHESTER: 35 KING STREET WEST
AGENTS IN ALL PRINCIPAL CENTRES

BUY A CAR MADE IN THE UNITED KINGDOM

AS162B

"*First* past the Traffic Lights!"

"My Fiat shot right ahead!
Acceleration's simply marvellous—that's where lightness tells. No wasted weight in the steel body, welded in one piece for greater strength. And the finish ! . . . Grand workmanship throughout. An engineer's job right down to the smallest detail. Absolutely reliable too—no trouble at all, though I'm always 'flogging' her. She stands up to it like a big car, and needs to, because once you step into the driver's seat you forget she's only a 'ten' costing but £198 !" I'd certainly get a Fiat if I were you !"

11 h.p. BALILLA De Luxe Saloon £198.   Open Sports £258.   15 h.p. ARDITA (4 cyl.) £295.

20 h.p. ARDITA (6 cyl.) De Luxe Saloon £395.   Sports Saloon £495.

1935   # FIAT

(ENGLAND) LIMITED
LANCELOT, RD., WEMBLEY

SOLE DISTRIBUTORS FOR LONDON & HOME COUNTIES : GORDON WATNEY & CO. LTD.   WEST END SHOWROOMS, 31, BROOK ST., LONDON, W.1.   PHONE: MAYFAIR 0267

11. h.p. BALILLA de Luxe Saloon £198.

FOR CATALOGUE—POST THIS COUPON
TO : FIAT (ENGLAND) LTD., LANCELOT RD.,WEMBLEY
Please send me catalogues giving full specifications and prices of the following Fiat models :
11 h.p. BALILLA ● BALILLA sports ● 15 & 17 h.p. ARDITA
20 h.p. ARDITA
(Kindly strike out models which do not interest you)

NAME ....

ADDRESS... *VOID*

174

1935

Performance —
and Comfort !

The great virtue of Sunbeam performance is the ease with which it is achieved. Smooth, silent power, exceptional acceleration, a perfect gearbox, progressively p o w e r f u l braking and incomparable ease of control. Whether in traffic or at speed on the open road the Sunbeam is a sheer delight to drive. And with this mechanical efficiency is combined the satisfying comfort of fine coachwork; perfectly proportioned lines, restful seating, clear vision for driver and passengers, and fittings and appointments designed for real convenience and not mere display. The experienced car owner who looks for " something better " finds that his search ends in the Sunbeam.

12.8 h.p., " Twenty," " Twenty-One Sports " and " Twenty-Five."

Prices from £425 to £1,045.

SUNBEAM
the best of the better cars

Dunlop tyres and wheels standard.

THE SUNBEAM MOTOR CAR COMPANY, LTD. (Russell Kettle, Receiver and Manager), MOORFIELD WORKS, WOLVERHAMPTON

A New **TICKFORD** *Model...*

1935

The 4-Light Coupe Cabriolet

on the **VAUXHALL Light Six £298**

AT Olympia you will see for the first time the new Tickford Coupe Cabriolet on the Vauxhall Motors Stand No 97. It has a new design easy-action drophead based on the famous Tickford principle. The action is entirely automatic. By simply releasing two spring fasteners and turning a small detachable handle in the rear panel, it is a matter of seconds only to change it from a completely closed saloon to an entirely open tourer. And the patent Tickford head is guaranteed indefinitely! Another advantage is the addition of rear quarter windows, giving plenty of light and excellent vision to passengers in the rear. The front seats are adjustable for legroom and the rear seat is fitted with a disappearing central arm rest. Pneumatic upholstery is fitted throughout. A roomy luggage boot is built in at the rear—the lid of this boot can be fixed horizontally to form a spacious luggage grid.

Price £298 on the Vauxhall Light Six
(12 h.p. or 14 h.p.)

Price £395 on the Vauxhall Big Six
(20 h.p. or 27 h.p.)

Full particulars from your local Vauxhall dealer or from Salmons & Sons, 13, New Burlington Street. London, W.1.
Works: Newport Pagnell, Bucks.

The Famous
TICKFORD
2-Light Drophead Coupe

is being shown at Olympia on the Salmons & Sons Stand No. **30**. This can quickly be converted from a completely closed coupe to a Coupe de Ville, and thence by turning a small detachable handle in the rear panel to an entirely open tourer.

VAUXHALL LIGHT SIX
TICKFORD COUPE, **£285**

VAUXHALL BIG SIX
TICKFORD COUPE, **£365**

With the head down this new Tickford Coupe Cabriolet is an entirely open Tourer.

MIDGET MG SERIES 'T'

1936

It's an M.G. Midget . . but with a difference! Engine is 10 h.p. rated. Chassis is underslung, bigger. Body and luggage space bigger. "Continental Grand Prix type" hydraulic brakes now. Fifteen-gallon petrol tank now, with three gallon reserve, dash operated. Maximum speed, acceleration, cornering . . all intensified now. A fine, fast, crack car—this latest Series 'T.' £222 ex works, two-seater form only. Dunlops. Triplex.

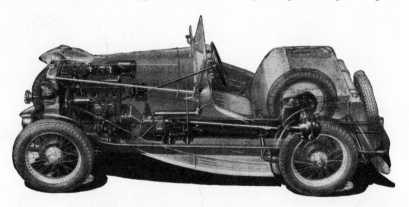

OTHER SPECIAL FEATURES : 1½ gallon air-cooled oil sump, with floating oil suction pipe and gauze : twin S.U. down-draught carburettors, and air silencer, air cleaner and fume consumer : thermostatic water cooling : heavy duty clutch running in oil : four-speed close ratio gearbox : Tecalemit chassis lubrication : two large capacity 6-volt batteries in series : large separate rev. counter and speedometer, and 8-day clock : rim-lit instruments : Dunlop centre lock 'Rudge' type wheels and 4.50" tyres.

THE M.G. CAR COMPANY LIMITED · ABINGDON-ON-THAMES · BERKSHIRE

BOSCH
famous in five continents

The strain and stress of modern racing demands super-reserve power coupled with far-reaching dependability . . . rock-firm and enduring. That is why the winners of the important races of 1936 insisted upon using Bosch plugs. Experience thus crystallized is to the perceptive motorist both his guide and guarantee . . . he says to his garage : "I must have BOSCH plugs."

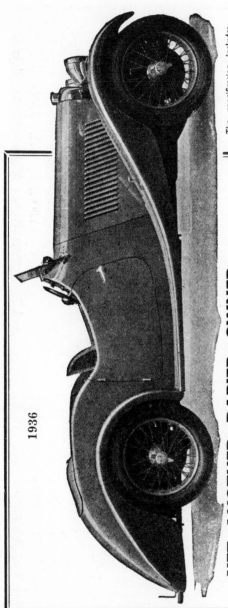

1936

YET ANOTHER RAPIER OWNER CONFIRMS OUR OPINION . . . . . .

This delighted Rapier owner, who has just taken delivery of his second Rapier Car, writes us concerning this new model:—

"......I have driven her back here and I was *delighted* with her performance, and the comfortable body. She feels more powerful than the older model and the engine is quieter. The body and springing are much more comfortable. I will write again when I have driven her more.........."

Yours truly,
(Sgnd) H. E. T. W.,
Cornwall.

The specification includes twin camshaft O.H.V. engine (1,100 c.c., Tax £7-10), E.N.V. 4-spd., preselector gears, Girling brakes, Dunlop tyres (Standard fitting) and full equipment. Streamline 4-seater Sports **£375** body .. .. ..

Prices performance run and particulars of other models upon request.

RAPIER

"EVER KEEN PERFORMANCE"

RAPIER CARS LTD., R.S.M. (Automobiles) LTD.,
195, Hammersmith Rd., London, W.6   26, Bruton St., Berkeley Square, W.1
'Phone: Riverside 3342 & 1008.   'Phone: Mayfair 0283.

Sole London Distributors:

"**That's** what I call PERFORMANCE!"

1936

IT'S easy to see why Hillman "SIXES" have been chosen for use in three important Government Departments — H.M. WAR OFFICE, THE ROYAL AIR FORCE and METROPOLITAN POLICE.

There could be no greater acknowledgment of their outstanding Performance and Dependability.

HILLMAN

"SIXTEEN" *Hawk* "80"

BUY A CAR MADE IN THE UNITED KINGDOM

From
£295
TRIPLEX GLASS
THROUGHOUT

BACKED BY WORLD-WIDE SERVICE – HILLMAN DEALERS ARE EVERYWHERE

THE HILLMAN MOTOR CAR CO. LTD., COVENTRY. *London Showrooms* and *Export Dept.* : ROOTES LTD., Devonshire House, Piccadilly, W.1

The
BRITISH
SALMSON

1936
SIX
CARS OF QUALITY

combining speed with economical running

1
12 H.P. 4-cylinder Close-Coupled Saloon
Seventy miles per hour
Thirty miles per gallon - - **£395**

2
12 H.P. 4-cylinder Full-Length Saloon
Seventy miles per hour
Thirty miles per gallon - **£395**

3
12 H.P. 4-cylinder Four-Seater Coupé
Seventy miles per hour
Thirty miles per gallon - **£395**

4
12 H.P. 4-cylinder Four-Seater Tourer
Seventy miles per hour
Thirty miles per gallon - - **£365**

5
20·8 H.P. 6-cylinder Two-Seater Sports
Ninety miles per hour
Twenty-three miles per gallon - **£645**

6
12 H.P. 4-cylinder Two-Seater Tourer
Eighty miles per hour
27/30 miles per gallon - - **£395**

The 20·8
TWO-SEATER SPORTS

with Independent Front Wheel
Suspension, and a speed of ninety
miles per hour, is a wonderful
combination of speed and control

BRITISH SALMSON
AERO ENGINES LTD.
RAYNES PARK, LONDON, S.W.20

We tried the others but.. we chose a VAUXHALL

1936

Your car cannot have all

these five outstanding features

unless it's a VAUXHALL

1 INDEPENDENT SPRINGING

Changes riding into gliding and provides the smoothest motoring ever experienced for back seat as well as front passengers.

2 CONTROLLED SYNCHRO-MESH

The Automatically Controlled Synchro-Mesh gear box means a faultless change. No pausing, no judging of engine speed—yet you cannot clash your gears.

3 NO-DRAUGHT VENTILATION

All the fresh air you want without draughts or rain beating in. Every passenger controls the ventilation in his or her part of the car.

4 BODY CONFORMITY SEATING

So form-fitting that it is as good as made-to-measure seating. Said to be the most comfortable car seat ever invented.

5 OUTSTANDING PERFORMANCE

10 m.p.h. to 30 m.p.h. — on top gear — in 10 1/5 secs. 10 m.p.h. to 30 m.p.h.—through the gears—in 5 4/5 secs. Stand to 50 m.p.h.— through the gears—in 20 secs. *vide AUTOCAR*

These 5 points and others . . . the smart modern lines, the inviting roomy interior . . . have made the Vauxhall Light Six popular everywhere. After comparing performance, comfort and *value* thousands of motorists have said, "We tried the others . . . but we chose a Vauxhall."

Ask Vauxhall owners—you must know some—what they think of their cars and the economy of running them. Their opinions will carry a lot more weight than what we say; then, to convince yourself that your choice is sound, make a real test of all the cars that interest you. Any Vauxhall dealer will be happy to put a car at your disposal.

LIGHT SIX

VAUXHALL LIGHT SIX 12 h.p. or 14 h.p. Six different body styles. Saloons from - - - - **£205**

Catalogues on request from Vauxhall Motors Limited, Luton, Beds. *If you want a bigger car there is the Vauxhall Big Six.* 20 h.p. or 27 h.p. *Prices from £325 to £550.*

THE RENAULT 17.9 H.P. 4 CYL.
SPORTS AIRLUXE SALOON £235

PERFORMANCE IN COMFORT

Even in these days, the successful combination of comfort and performance is rarely found at anything like the low prices of the Renault Airluxe models. Whether you buy the 12 H.P. Saloon at £215, *including 4-wheel jacks*, or the powerful 17.9 H.P. at £235, you will obtain a high performance motor car with interior roominess out of all proportion to the size of the chassis. The back seat of either saloon, for example, provides 4" more width than "The Motor" have pronounced to be the *BIG CAR IDEAL*

1936

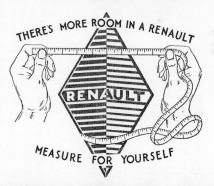

THERE'S MORE ROOM IN A RENAULT

RENAULT

MEASURE FOR YOURSELF

RENAULT LIMITED
Western Avenue,
London, W.3
(Acorn 4655)

West End Showrooms:
21, Pall Mall,
London, S.W.1
(Whitehall 7270)

RENAULT

Laurels AGAIN !
SCOTTISH RALLY
(Coachwork Competition)
1st PRIZE CLASS I OPEN CARS
2nd PRIZE CLASS II OPEN CARS

1936

AVON

FLYING LIGHT TEN £239
FLYING LIGHT TWELVE £245
FLYING TWELVE - £335
FLYING SIXTEEN - £365
FLYING TWENTY - £370

THE NEW AVON BODY CO. LTD. WARWICK ENGLAND

3½-Litre Drophead Coupe £665—
saloon or completely open car in
five seconds—one man operated.

WHERE TO SEE
George Brough's NEW
3½ LITRE DURING THE SHOW

Owing to the fact that Brough Superior Cars Ltd. (as distinct from Brough Superior Motor Cycles) have not been registered as Motor Car Manufacturers for the length of time required by the S.M.M.T. Show Regulations, we are unable to exhibit at Olympia this year. Fortunately, however, there will be every opportunity to inspect, during the Show, the new Brough 3½-Litre at the Showrooms of our London Distributors, Messrs. Kevill-Davies and March Ltd., and at those of our other Brough Superior Distributors. There will also be available Brough Superior Models for demonstrations and trial runs during this period.

1936

I have no hesitation in saying that I have produced in the 3½-Litre a 6-Cylinder car whose performance compares more than favourably with that of the 8-Cylinder Brough Superior. The attraction of driving the 3½-Litre lies, I think, not so much in its speed (though this must surely be unequalled by any 6-Cylinder car of normal tuning), but in the cumulative effect of fast, silent, and very comfortable travel, with perfect response at all times from a powerful, well balanced engine. You will find a test of this car an extremely satisfying experience.

The 3½-Litre Brough Superior is individually built by craftsmen who have made the name Brough famous throughout the world during the past 20 years.

The particular grade of Speedwell Oils mentioned in the Driving Instruction Booklet, is exclusively recommended to be used in Brough Superior Cars.

Brough Superior

BROUGH SUPERIOR CARS
Tel.: Nottingham 65535/6

LTD., HAYDN RD., NOTTS.
Grams & Cables: Brufsup, Nottm.

SOLE DISTRIBUTORS FOR LONDON AND THE HOME COUNTIES:—
KEVILL-DAVIES & MARCH LTD., 28, Berkeley Street, Berkeley Square, London, W.1

DISTRIBUTORS FOR OTHER PARTS OF THE BRITISH ISLES:

SCOTLAND:	YORKS., NORTHUMBERLAND & DURHAM:	HANTS., WILTS & DORSET:
Messrs. G. C. Macandrew & Co. Ltd., 86, Lothian Road, Edinburgh.	F. W. Dixon, Linthorpe Road, Middlesbrough.	Messrs. Ewens Motors, 1, Lansdowne Road, Bournemouth.
CHANNEL ISLANDS:	LANCASHIRE:	NOTTINGHAMSHIRE:
Messrs. G. H. Pool & Sons Ltd., 21, Burrard Street, Jersey.	Messrs. Frasers Ltd., 65, Great Moor Street, Bolton.	Messrs. C. H. Truman Ltd., Mansfield Road, Nottingham.

STAFFS., WARWS., WORC., GLOS. & MON.: Messrs. The Motor House, 59, John Bright Street, Birmingham.

The DROP-HEAD COUPE
£695

1936

"The Acceleration of the Lammas Really Astounded Me!"

says BOBBY HOWES

Internationally famous Stage and Screen Star

"I had a 'pre-view' of the Lammas a few days before the Show opened. In all my motoring experience I have never been more impressed by the performance of any motor car than I was by this. It is almost incredible!" Mr. Bobby Howes is a keen motorist with considerable experience of high-speed continental touring and his motor cars have always been representative of the world's finest. His appreciation of the Lammas-Graham's performance and the very favourable impression which he gained of its unusually complete equipment is, then, worthy confirmation of the manufacturer's belief that this motor car will definitely appeal to the discerning motorist—the motorist who demands a combination of luxurious, silent comfort and quite exceptional performance. The Lammas will reach "50" in single figure seconds from zero and still have speed to spare at "90." At the same time, it is a distinguished "town carriage."

Sole London Distributors:
CHARLES FOLLETT LTD.,
18, BERKELEY STREET, W.1.

LAMMAS LIMITED,
HEAD OFFICE AND SALES DEPT.,
32, ST. MARY ABBOT'S TERRACE,
LONDON, W.14.

SALOON: £660   TOURER: £620

THE LAMMAS - GRAHAM

"A Car Built to a New Ideal"

189

THE CONCENSUS OF EXPERT OPINION—

"A Truly Remarkable Car!"

1936

—*The Autocar*

The new "Sportsline" Coachbuilt Saloon

The specification of the FRAZER-NASH-B.M.W. includes many features which must appeal to the enthusiast ; among others, exceptional power-to-weight ratio ; high gear ratios ; perfect steering ; remarkable steering lock ; excellent driving position and independent suspension and steering, giving amazing road-holding and cornering.

"Knowing something of the fame of this car I was prepared to find it really good, and I was not disappointed. I left Liverpool via the Mersey tunnel and headed for North Wales, although I had been warned that the roads were covered with ice and frozen snow. By the time I had cleared the restricted areas I felt absolutely at home on the car. **The response to the throttle was instantaneous and the acceleration was amazing.**

"The steering was first-class, being high-geared yet light, it enabled the driver to place the car to the proverbial inch.

"**At all speeds the engine is dead quiet, absolutely smooth, and enabled the driver to put up high averages in absolute safety** with the minimum of fatigue.

"With the perfect weight distribution and independent springing and steering in front, the **FRAZER-NASH-B.M.W. sits on the road in a simply remarkable manner.** Corners and open bends can be taken as fast as the driver's courage will permit him to drive at them, with never a sign of body sway or inclination to slide. I can safely say I have never driven a car faster on bends, or with such confidence. This stability, allied with the perfect steering and first-class brakes, gives the driver

a margin of safety that is very large, and in an emergency the same quality is worth more than anything else a driver could desire.

"On the frozen roads, covered alternatively with packed snow, sheet ice and axle-deep slush, I never experienced a single skid. I found it possible to drive under these conditions at least 20 m.p.h. faster than I would have attempted on a normally sprung car. It is difficult, having driven this FRAZER-NASH-B.M.W., not to indulge in superlatives. I have spoken to many experienced drivers who have handled it and without exception they praise it wholeheartedly.

"It is perhaps on pot-holed roads and level crossings that one appreciates the springing most. These hazards can be crossed at astonishingly high speeds with never the slightest jar either to the front or back seat passengers.

"The clutch is light and very sweet—the car will pull away from 6 to 7 m.p.h. on top very rapidly. **The FRAZER-NASH-B.M.W. is a sheer delight to handle.**"

—*The Birkenhead News.*

Read the experts—readers of " Speed " are invited to send for a new illustrated leaflet containing an interesting selection of road-test reports and other literature

A.F.N. LTD. London Road, Isleworth, Middlesex
32, Grosvenor Street, Mayfair, W.1

S-S-S-SH!

..... fit a 1936

VORTEX
SILENCER

This Scientific Silencing System Ensures

MORE POWER—QUICKER ACCELERATION—COOLER ENGINE—LOWER FUEL CONSUMPTION—SILENCE WITHOUT BACK PRESSURE

★ *Ask your Garage or write direct to:—*
**LAYCOCK ENGINEERING CO. LTD.,
MILLHOUSES, SHEFFIELD.**

REF. N.M.N.

fit a "CAR PUP"

The disadvantages associated with the ordinary trailer are entirely absent in the "CAR PUP." The castor wheel makes manœuvring or reversing easy. The "CAR PUP" can be easily and instantly detached.

WRITE FOR ILLUSTRATED FOLDER

and forget all luggage troubles!

You need no longer bung your car up with luggage, golf clubs, rugs or camping equipment; you can tow them behind in the "CAR PUP," where they will be absolutely safe and dry. The patent rigid coupling ensures perfect stability.

LAYCOCK ENGINEERING Co. Ltd. (Dept. C), **MILLHOUSES, SHEFFIELD.**

Folk who value their money adequately decide, in ever-increasing numbers, on the

£100

1936 FORD SALOON

(£6 TAX IN GREAT BRITAIN),

Britain's first £100 Saloon, really completely equipped, incomparably the best bargain in motor cars produced entirely in the United Kingdom. Comfort, speed, performance generally, appearance (*lastingly* good, inside and out) and economy of running and maintenance, surprise everybody who examines it, tries it on the road.

 1936 OLYMPIC GAMES, BERLIN, AUG. 1—15 NEXT.

Touring information really valuable to Ford owners visiting Germany for the outstanding athletic festival of the year may be obtained upon application.

As illustrated, £100. Double-Entrance Saloon, £112 . 10s. Hide Upholstery and Sliding Roof, £10 Extra, on Either Model.

Literature on Request : All Prices at Works : Dealers Everywhere

FORD CARS, FORDSON VANS & TRUCKS— PROVED BY THE PAST—IMPROVED FOR THE FUTURE!

FORD MOTOR COMPANY LIMITED, DAGENHAM, ESSEX.   LONDON SHOWROOMS : 88 REGENT STREET, W.1

ESCAPE FROM MONOTONY!

of the mass - produced car

1933 Olympia, Fitzmaurice Streamline Saloon (12 h.p. Tatra)
" . . . . the Fitzmaurice streamlined . . . . saloon contains much that is logical and common-sense." Vide THE TIMES, October 7th, 1933.

1934 Olympia, Fitzmaurice " Airstream " Saloon (11 h.p. Singer)
" . . . . Known as the Fitzmaurice, the body especially gives a great gain in performance efficiency . . . . other features make it a striking advance on conventional design." Vide THE NEWS CHRONICLE, July 13th, 1934.

1935 Austria Steyr 50
" Allows exceptional passenger space . . . . . . nothing to suggest ' cheapness.' . . . ."
Vide THE AUTOCAR, August 28th, 1936.

1936 " . . . . Fitzmaurice . . . . most recent designs . . . . . be accepted as beautiful by people who design pottery or jewellery."
Vide THE AUTOCAR, August 28th, 1936.

NOW!! FITZMAURICE CARS announce orders can be accepted for ultra-modern low air resistance super-luxury saloon cars (illustrated below). Produced in limited series by highly skilled hand workmanship of first-quality materials, with modern architectural treatment of exterior and interior form, utilising the most modern modified chassis bases, the whole constitutes the modern car in its most perfect form. End to end clean running streaming contours save petrol, power, tyre, engine and transmission wear. Eddy-free forepart, safety panoramic outlook, luxurious comfort and increased spaciousness, and other novel, common-sense advanced features are incorporated.

1936

30 h.p. 5-6-seater 6-window 4-door saloon. Price **£495**

ON VIEW AT

FORD MOTOR EXHIBITION

EXHIBITED BY
H. E. NUNN & CO. LTD.

10 h.p. 4-5-seater
4-window, 4-door saloon
Price **£335**

Write for literature only to:
FITZMAURICE CARS

122A, HIGH STREET - - LONDON, N.W.8   'Phone : Primrose 6877

The Roominess & Comfort of a large saloon with the Appearance & Performance of a Sportsman's Car

1936

The Wolseley 14/56 h.p. Saloon has proved to be one of the most successful cars ever made in this country. Ask anybody who owns one.

ROOMINESS. The Wolseley 14/56 seats 5 grown-up people in armchair comfort—plenty of elbow room, ample head-clearance and generous leg stretch.

COMFORT. Large-section extra low pressure Dunlops—long auto-lubricated semi-elliptical springs controlled by hydraulic shock absorbers, anatomical seating and sound insulation ensure a smooth and silent ride.

FRESH AIR. Cleverly planned draughtless ventilation (akin to air-conditioning), keeps the atmosphere fresh and free from fumes.

EASE OF DRIVING. Finger-light controls, synchromesh gears, adjustable steering and a clear wide view of the road with no blind spots.

PERFORMANCE. "Autocar" data gives top speed as 70.87 m.p.h. You reach 50 m.p.h. from rest in 24 secs. You can brake to a standstill from 30 m.p.h. in 30 feet. Speed is smooth, effortless driving free of fatigue and strain.

PRICE. £265 ex works. Tax £10.10. 24 to 28 m.p.g.

WOLSELEY RANGE. 10/40 h.p. saloon and coupe. Prices from £220. 12/48 h.p. saloon and coupé. Prices from £225. 14/56 h.p. saloon £265. 14/56 Salon de ville £295. 16 h.p., 21 h.p. and 25 h.p. Super Sixes. Prices from £325. 25 h.p. Salon de ville £425. 25 h.p. Sportsman's saloon £425. 25 h.p. Limousine £725. Prices ex works.

BUY WISELY - BUY **WOLSELEY**

THE TRUSTWORTHY CAR

Wolseley Motors Ltd., Ward End, Birmingham 8. London Distributors : Eustace Watkins Ltd., Berkeley St., W.1. Sole Exporters : M. I. E. Ltd., Cowley, Oxford, Eng.

DON'T STRUGGLE WITH THE STARTER!

1936

In the early cold winter's morning, after your car has been in the garage all night—or parked during severest frost—you can enjoy **Instant Starting** and a **Quick Getaway** by fitting a "SOLEX" Carburettor. Improved performance and a reduction in petrol consumption is certain and you will save your batteries too.

Fit your car with "SOLEX" NOW—
Winter is imminent.

FIT THE
SELF-STARTING
SOLEX
CARBURETTOR

Write for full details of our
30 Days' FREE TRIAL OFFER
without obligation to purchase.

SOLEX LIMITED
(Director—Gordon Richards)
SOLEX WORKS, 223-231, MARYLEBONE ROAD,
LONDON, N.W.1.

Telephones:
Paddington 5011 (6 lines).

Telegrams:
"Solexcarb, Norwest, London."

FREE TRIAL OFFER COUPON

My car is :—Make...

H.P..........Year..........

Please send price of Self-Starting "Solex" to suit and details of your 30 Days' Free Trial Offer.

Name......................... VOID ....

Address...

Post to SOLEX LTD., SOLEX WORKS, 223-231, MARYLEBONE RD., LONDON, N.W.1.

GOODBYE TO "Cramped-up" MOTORING!

1936

Roomy, certainly ... but a magnificent performer as well!

THE "KESTREL" (as illustrated)

Two-cylinder horizontally opposed water-cooled 7-h.p. engine (the now famous Jowett "flat twin" design) 3-point suspended on hydraulic mountings. The mounting at the forward end, specially designed by Jowett, absorbs the lightest possible engine vibration. Equipment includes opening windscreen, Luvax hydraulic shock absorbers, rear petrol tank with pump feed, petrol gauge, clock, Magna wheels, front and rear bumpers. Price **£165**

THE "FALCON" Saloon - - £152 10.
THE "FLYING FOX" Two-Seater - £158
THE "WEASEL" Sports Tourer - £165
All prices Ex Works
ANNUAL TAX £5.5.0

Take every measurement you can to prove "roominess" and the Jowett comes out far and away ahead as the roomiest light car on the road. You can really stretch your legs out and loll back in comfort in the rear as well as the front seats. There's plenty of luggage room, too. And in performance, like all its predecessors, this year's Jowett "has the legs" of every other light car at the same price. Before you question that statement remember that the unique Jowett "Flat Twin" engine gives a far more favourable power-to-weight ratio than orthodox design. That's why "big car" coachwork can be built on a car with an engine taxed at £5.5.0.

Also this year — for those wanting *extra* performance — there is the 10-h.p. Jowett "Flat Four" — with a horizontally opposed four-cylinder engine built on traditional Jowett lines.

JOWETT

THE *Roomiest* LIGHT CAR

1937

Always fast - but never flurried!

ONLY after arrival do you realise the speed at which
you came . . . . in this silent and luxurious "15/98"
Aston Martin. For out of a brilliant racing tradition has been
created a new entity. With a silky-smooth engine developing its
power so sweetly, the luxury of this car irresistibly reminds
you of a limousine . . . . that is capable of well over 80 m.p.h.
Open Four-Seater £575. Saloon £595. Speed Chassis (105
m.p h.) £695.

NEW "15/98" h.p.

ASTON-MARTIN

fast luxury

ASTON MARTIN LTD. FELTHAM, MIDDLESEX.   PHONE: FELTHAM 2291

FLASHING TO FAME !

CADET, 11·3 h.p
From
£135

OLYMPIA, 11·3 h.p.
From
£155

2-litre Saloon,
4-door.
£205

2½-litre Saloon.
£225

1937

OPEL

BIG CAR LUXURY AT SMALL CAR COST

leads on

- PERFORMANCE
- DEPENDABILITY
- PRICE & DESIGN
- EQUIPMENT
- ROOMY COMFORT

Foursome
Drop-head
Coupe.
£265

PRIDE & CLARKE LTD.

DISTRIBUTORS FOR LONDON & SOUTH EASTERN COUNTIES
237, BRIXTON HILL, S.W.2 Tulse Hill 6211   **107, PARK LANE, W.I** Grosvenor 2708

A FEW MAIN DEALERS AND THEIR ADDRESSES:

Brighton—G.A. Motors, 50, St. James's Street.
Bucks.—Station Garages, Ltd., Amersham.
Chelmsford—Chelmsford Car Services, Chelmer Road.
Colchester—Candor Motors, Ltd., Malden Road.
Croydon—West Croydon Motors, Ltd., 399, London Road.
Epsom—Page Motors, Ltd., 78, High Street.
Folkestone—Auto Pilots, Ltd., The Harbour Garage.
Gt. Yarmouth—Johnston's Garage, 60, Northgate Street.
Guildford—Puttock's, Ltd., High Street.
Hunts.—Ireland Bros., St. Neots.
Ipswich—W. J. Coe, Ltd., Crown Street.

Kent—Northwood Garages, Tankerton.
London,—Grand Garages, Ltd.,GunnersburyAve., W.5, and 305, Richmond Rd.,E.Twickenham.
London—Tankard & Smith, Ltd., 363, Bromley Road, S.E.6.
Lowestoft—Day's Garage, 69a, London North Road.
Luton—Millward & Co., Beech Hill.
Maidstone—Anstey's Garages, Ltd., 30/34, Stone Street.
Northampton—Rolls Motor Co., Kingsley Park Garage.
Norwich—Maude St. Faichs, Ltd., Cromer Road.
Old Windsor—Friary Motors, Ltd, Straight Rd.

Peterborough—The Broadway Garage.
Reading—Reading Garages, Ltd., Cork Street.
Rickmansworth—Wright's Motors, Ltd., Park Garage.
Saffron Walden—Raynham & Co., Ltd.
Slough—Fullbrook & Co. (Slough), Ltd., Fullbrook House.
Waltham Cross—Broadley Garage, Ltd., Nazeing.
Wembley—Stadium Motors, Ltd., Wembley Hill Road.
West Byfleet—Byfleet Automobile Engineering Co., Ltd., Old Woking Road.
Westcliff-on-Sea—Chalkwell Car-Exchange, 686, London Road.

A PRODUCT OF GENERAL MOTORS

LOOK *at these deeply moulded slots. On wet or dry roads, a touch of the brake presses open these slots, allowing the rubber ridges in between to grip the road like strong sinewy fingers.*

1937

SLIPPERY ROADS MADE SAFE BY THIS SLOTTED TREAD—A PROVED AND EXCLUSIVE ENGLEBERT FEATURE

No recent innovation—this wonderful Englebert A.D. tread—but a design proved by years of gruelling test and success on Continental road and track.

No shallow cuts but deep moulded slots which defy wear and hold their incomparable non-skid properties right to the very end of the tyre's long life.

Continental drivers choose Engleberts for touring on rough roads and racing on the fastest circuits. The toughened rubber tread gives an amazing long life on English Roads.

Silent on all surfaces, the Englebert A.D. is the master-tyre of today. Next time replace with Englebert. Get more miles and lasting safety.

Write for free sample block showing the A. D. non-skid tread.

ENGLEBERT
A.D. TYRES

ENGLEBERT TYRES LTD., 162 GT. PORTLAND ST., LONDON, W.1, and at Bristol Liverpool, Leeds and Edinburgh. Factories in Belgium.

1937

THE CAR WITH *Both* THE ANSWERS

Treat it, if you like, as a supremely comfortable means of transport — smooth and silent and restful — at home with the dignity of Berkeley Square. But treat it, too, as a sportsman's car, really at its best when it's flying down the Great North Road. Whatever you look for in a car, you'll find the answer in this 2-litre Frazer-Nash-B.M.W. 65 m.p.h. all day, with 80 when you want it. The comfort that comes from independent springing. Exceptional road-holding and striking acceleration. Is it to be a luxurious saloon — or a true sports car? . . . Here is the car with *both* the answers.

Type 326 five-seater 4-door Saloon. Price (with cloth upholstery) £475. Price (with leather upholstery) £495. Also available as a five-seater drop-head Cabriolet. Price £575.

FRAZER - NASH - B.M.W

JOINT LONDON DISTRIBUTORS

L. C. BINGHAM, LTD.,
32 GROSVENOR ST., LONDON, W.1
Telephone: Mayfair 7972 (3 lines)

FRAZER-NASH CARS,
FALCON WORKS, ISLEWORTH
Telephone: Hounslow 0011 (4 lines)

George Brough

INTRODUCES HIS ★ 1938

 Brough Superior $3\frac{1}{2}$ - LITRE MODEL

George Brough (known for his remarkable motorcycles) has produced another even more interesting car. Satisfying in proportion and line, the 1938 Brough Superior offers noteworthy performance with perfect road holding and controlled steering even at the high speeds of which it is capable. (For the Alpine Sports model, the "Motor"'s official figures were: standing mile, 94 m.p.h., 0-50 m.p.h. in 7 1/5 secs.) It is also of interest to note that the standard Brough Superior is fitted with a patent Dual Purpose body, convertible from Tourer to Saloon in 5 seconds by one person.

The Brough Superior $3\frac{1}{2}$-litre 22 h.p. models.

Dual Purpose Drophead Coupe de Luxe, 4-seater £665

As above but supercharged £775

Alpine Grand Sports (supercharged) - £845

Saloon, 4-door, double sliding roof - - £695

Brough Superior

★ DURING THE SHOW we shall be happy to arrange demonstrations of the Brough Superior models at the Showrooms of

Sole Distributors for London and the Home Counties

THE MOTOR COMBINE

365 Euston Road, London, N.W.1.

'Phone: EUSton 4141

BROUGH SUPERIOR CARS LIMITED, NOTTINGHAM

Telephone: 5535/6 Nottingham.   Telegrams and Cables: Brufsup, Nottingham.

204

CANADA CALLING
BRITAIN to Buy

1937

THE CANADIAN
CHEVROLET

★ 1,168,570 CHEVROLETS WERE SOLD LAST YEAR

Search throughout the Empire — the streets of London, the African veldt, the Australian bush and the mountain ranges of Canada — everywhere Chevrolet predominates. The reason is not far to seek. Chevrolet is an Empire car built in the great Chevrolet factories at Oshawa, Canada. Pound for pound it offers the greatest motoring value obtainable in the world to-day — in safety, brilliant performance and sheer luxurious comfort it has no peer at anything like its price.

MASTER SALOONS FROM
£268

Sole Concessionaires for the United Kingdom:

PASS and JOYCE LTD., Chevrolet House, (By Selfridge's) 24-27, Orchard Street, W.1. - Phone : MAYfair 5141

BUY A CANADIAN CHEVROLET

now from
£149

THE WORLD'S ROOMIEST, SAFEST, MOST ECONOMICAL 8.H.P. CAR   1938

D.K.W. models down in price! At a time of rising costs that's *real* news — and at its now reduced price of £149 the Auto-Union D.K.W. model offers more remarkable value than ever. But the price is the only thing that is changed. With ample room for four people, exceptional road-holding and 45 m.p.g. guaranteed, the Auto-Union D.K.W. model is still the safest, most economical 8 h.p. car in the world. Drive one yourself and prove it!

FLEXIBILITY
The flexibility of the D.K.W. in top gear makes driving in traffic exceptionally easy. Gear-changing is simplicity itself.

SAFETY
Road - holding of which " The Motor" says "severe open bends can be taken at nearly 60 m.p.h. with complete safety" make this the safest of all light cars.

ECONOMY
"The Motor" test of the D.K.W. showed 47 m.p.g. when driven hard, and 45 m.p.g. is guaranteed. How does that compare with your present car?

SPACIOUSNESS
There is really generous room for four full-sized people and a very roomy luggage boot. Wide doors make for easy access to the rear seats.

AUTO-UNION SALES LTD., 151-153 GT. PORTLAND STREET, LONDON, W.1.

3½ litre

JENSEN

2¼ litre   A CAR BUILT IN THE UNITED KINGDOM

THE Earl of Cardigan, writing in "Britannia & Eve," says:—"The 'Jensen' . . . . . may be described as both impressive and intriguing . . . . an unusual and distinctive proposition. A first-rate engine—and a chassis which enables high speeds to be maintained with perfect confidence . . . ." With the 'Jensen' preselective over-drive, it is possible "to cruise at anything up to 85 m.p.h. with an extraordinary degree of silence, economy and ease . . . . ." Consider these figures :—90 m.p.h., 22 m.p.g., 6-ratio gearbox, only 2,000 r.p.m. at 60 m.p.h. 3½-litre models with preselective overdrive from £645. 2¼-litre models from £495.

Send for full details and Road Tests of this unique motor-car.

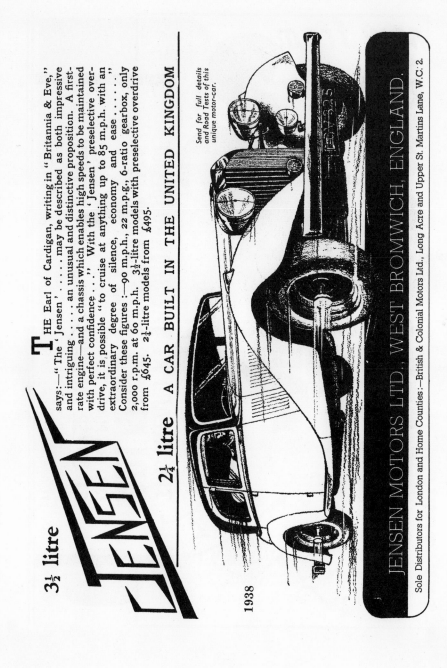

1938

1 INDEPENDENT FRONT WHEEL SPRINGING

2 HIGH POWER-WEIGHT RATIO

3 LOW CENTRE OF GRAVITY

4 DAIMLER FLUID FLYWHEEL TRANSMISSION
Licensed under Vulcan-Sinclair & Daimler patents

1938

In **ONE CAR** *for the* *first time*

5 SEPARATE ENCLOSED LUGGAGE COMPARTMENT

6 ADJUSTABLE STEERING COLUMN

7 INTER-AXLE SEATING

8 ACCESSIBLE ENCLOSED SPARE WHEEL

9 RUBBER-MOUNTED REAR SPRINGS

10 PERFECT VENTILATION OBTAINED WITHOUT PIVOTING WINDOWS

11 HAND-BRAKE FITTED JUST BENEATH DASH ON OFFSIDE

12 FLEXIBLY MOUNTED ENGINE

13 THERMOSTATICALLY CONTROLLED COOLING

14 QUICK ACTING LIFT-UP BONNET

15 LARGE ANTI-ROLL CONTROL BARS FRONT AND REAR

16 INSULATED EXHAUST SYSTEM

What are the things about other cars that have struck you as desirable? List them—then check them off against this new Lanchester.

For in this remarkable car every single worth-while feature has been incorporated.

The result is a car that makes motoring a rare pleasure. It floats you over the worst roads (independent front wheel springing). It gets you away from traffic hold-ups ahead of the rest (high power-weight ratio). It corners at speed—even on a false camber—sitting well down on the road, with no suggestion of roll (low centre of gravity and anti-roll control). An untiring car for both driver and passengers—the Daimler Fluid Flywheel Transmission cuts the driver's work to a minimum and gives the smooth-running engine an even greater smoothness.

Truly the new Lanchester Roadrider De Luxe is a joy to drive and a pride to own.

The new **LANCHESTER** *Roadrider* ◆ DE-LUXE

LANCHESTER 6-CYLINDER '14' ROADRIDER DE LUXE
from **£365** *Tax £10.10*

FOR £25 LESS you can have the same car with synchro-mesh gearbox and ordinary clutch.

'Eighteen' from £525 'Roadrider' from £330 'Eleven' from £275
British Cars Last Longer

THE LANCHESTER MOTOR CO. LTD., COVENTRY. LONDON DISTRIBUTORS: THE CAR MART LTD., 3/5 BURLINGTON GARDENS, W.1

WHY
3 Generations
HAVE PURCHASED MERCEDES - BENZ

When a factory from its earliest days of production and without interruption to the present time has accomplished outstanding performances on road and track with its productions, such can only be regarded as development in its fullest sense.

At the same time it also signifies the value which is obtainable in the standard productions of the Mercedes-Benz factory.

Such success has always been the basis as well for further achievements and developments which, in their turn, have proved of the greatest service towards constructional perfection of the car in everyday use.

SUCH IS MERCEDES-BENZ

Grandfather purchased because of our " Grand-Prix " success

Father purchased because of our victory at the " Targo-Floria "

The Son purchased a Mercedes-Benz because he knew he would benefit from the outstanding success achieved both on Road and Track throughout the year.

1939

MERCEDES·BENZ

BRITISH MERCEDES-BENZ LIMITED, 110, Park Lane, London, W.1. Mayfair 5555

The confidence of
1938   driving a $\mathcal{D}$aimler

You feel secure at the wheel of a Daimler. Daimler steering is very light : yet the car obeys it as accurately as a muscle obeys the mind. You miss no heart-beats, handling a Daimler, when emergency calls for a sudden stop or a quick move ahead. Daimler response to brake or throttle is immediate, unflurried, sure. You drive at your ease on rough, wet roads in a car that neither bumps nor pitches — that takes its corners without a trace of roll. You drive without strain in congested city traffic, with a gear control that leaves both hands for the wheel. Physical comfort — certainty — peace of mind : there's solid confidence in driving a Daimler.

By Appointment
to His Majesty the late
King George V

'THE MOST INTERESTING CAR OF THE YEAR'

Sports Saloon £485

THE NEW

$\mathcal{D}$aimler

`FIFTEEN´
16.2 H.P.
SIX-LIGHT SALOON £475

- **Independent front wheel springing**

- **Anti-roll control bars front and rear**

- **Inter-axle seating. Positive steering**

- **Daimler Fluid Flywheel Transmission with pre-selective self-changing gearbox**
  (Licensed under Vulcan-Sinclair and Daimler Patents)

British cars last longer

THE DAIMLER COMPANY LIMITED, COVENTRY.   LONDON DISTRIBUTORS : STRATSTONE. 27, PALL MALL, & 38, BERKELEY ST.

Super Snipe Sports Saloon £430

" . . . at last a British manufacturer is producing a car which satisfies our peculiar tastes and requirements, and, at the same time, possesses a top-gear performance which, in all its aspects, is, in my opinion, superior to that of any foreign product."

Mr. Sidney Henschel, Financial News, 23rd February, 1939.

HUMBER 1939

THE SIXTEEN	THE SNIPE	THE SUPER SNIPE	THE IMPERIAL	THE PULLMAN
from £345	from £355	from £385	from £515	from £750

HUMBER LTD., COVENTRY. *London Showrooms & Export Division :* ROOTES LTD., DEVONSHIRE HOUSE, PICCADILLY, W.I

The sale of Sunbeam-Talbot Cars is greater than ever before in the history of both Companies, the increase even over the previous record year is 38.6%.

Such popularity _Must_ be deserved!

Try a Sunbeam-Talbot to-day!

1939

THE 'TEN' from £250   '4 LITRE' SPORTS SALOON £525   THE '3 LITRE' from £415

SUNBEAM-TALBOT LTD., LONDON, W.10

World Exporters: Rootes Ltd., Devonshire House, Piccadilly, W.1.   London Showrooms: Warwick Wright Ltd., 150 New Bond Street, W.1

GREAT DRIVE ON ALL FRONTS

1939

The greatest drive of all is located at the front of every CITROËN. Great because it kills the motorists' bogey . . . skidding ! Great because it makes high-speed cornering safe ! And CITROËN front drive is allied to a lively o.h.v. engine that saves you money . . . because the replaceable cylinder barrels eliminate rebores, reduce oil consumption and improve cooling. There is a one-piece welded steel body to provide the safest and strongest of all designs, with torsion bar springing and independent wheel suspension combining to give the most luxurious riding of our time. Experience it yourself by asking your dealer for a trial run.

★ *In 1934 Citroën introduced* INTEGRAL ALL-STEEL BODY AND CHASSIS. TORSION BAR SPRINGING. FRONT-WHEEL DRIVE. INDEPENDENT FRONT WHEEL SUSPENSION. REPLACEABLE CYLINDER BARRELS. FACIA-BOARD GEAR-CHANGE. FLOOR DESIGN FREE OF CONTROLS, FOOTWELLS AND TUNNELS.

Prices and Models

"Twelve" Saloon - - -	£238
Popular Saloon - - -	£198
Roadster - - - -	£265
"Light Fifteen" Saloon -	£248
Popular Saloon - - -	£208
Roadster - - - -	£275
"Big Fifteen" Saloon - -	£278
7-seater Saloon - - -	£298

CITROËN

CITROËN CARS · LTD · SLOUGH · BUCKS

Fine Cars those *FIATS* !

That's the TEN-TWELVE!

It's easy to pick out those Fiats—by their distinctive design, by their slick style, by their flashing performance! Who's first away when the lights turn green? The fellow in the Fiat! Who does over 68 in top and over 32 to the gallon with a 10-horse Saloon? The fellow in the Fiat!

Compare the Fiat 10/12 with any other "ten" you like, point for point and feature for feature. You'll find it the best value for money on the road to-day. If it's a smaller car you want, go for the famous Fiat "500"—the little car with the big behaviour.

FACTS AND FEATURES OF THE FIAT 10/12.

- *4-cylinder overhead valve engine with aluminium head.*
- *4-speeds synchromesh.*
- *Special independent front-wheel suspension.*
- *Independent steering control to each front wheel.*
- *Hydraulic brakes and shock absorbers to all four wheels.*
- *All-metal body, four doors, without central pillar. Aerodynamic design.*
- *Over 68 M.P.H. More than 32 m.p.g.*
- *Disc wheels and extra low pressure tyres.*
- *Down-draught carburetter with easy-starting device.*
- *Air cleaner and silencer.*
- *Large luggage boot. Leather upholstery throughout.*

PRICE £198 FIXED HEAD SALOON
(Sliding Roof £10 extra).

Note complete absence of centre door-pillars, allowing easy entry or exit, especially to rear seats

1939

FIAT
for *Performance!*

FIAT (England) Ltd., Water Road, Wembley, Middlesex. *Perivale 5651.*
London Showrooms: Hanover Motors Ltd., 12, Princes Street, Hanover Sq., W.1. Telephone: MAYfair 8691.

298 GNS.

never bought
so much in
car value

1939

1½ Litre Dolomite Saloon 298 Gns.
(Wheel discs extra)

A well-known motor critic recently wrote :—" The coachwork is very distinctive—the equipment is lavish—this car is of very definite individuality, standing aloof in its every respect from the mass-produced type of vehicle.

" It can reach 80 m.p.h.—rev. up to 60 m.p.h. on third for overtaking purposes—climbs hills fast or slow as desired and its behaviour throughout is firm—it steers to a hair, it brakes smoothly and powerfully, it accelerates definitely and evenly, and it rides well. In a word, it claims all the hall-marks of quality.

" In this particular niche of the market the Triumph-Dolomite has no superiors. It is a vehicle which any enthusiast can be proud to own."

May we arrange a demonstration to suit your convenience entirely without obligation and send you our beautiful art catalogue illustrating and describing the complete range of models?

TRIUMPH-DOLOMITE

The Smartest Cars in the Land

TRIUMPH COMPANY LTD., COVENTRY. *London Showrooms:* **28, Albemarle St., W.1**

The 'Prefect' 1939

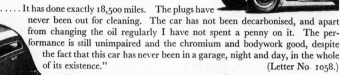

".... It has done exactly 18,500 miles. The plugs have never been out for cleaning. The car has not been decarbonised, and apart from changing the oil regularly I have not spent a penny on it. The performance is still unimpaired and the chromium and bodywork good, despite the fact that this car has never been in a garage, night and day, in the whole of its existence." (Letter No. 1058.)

beats the lot,

"I beg to bring to your notice that my Ford has done 34,467 miles in 15 months : it has cost me nothing in repairs. I am bringing this to your notice, as this is the fourth Ford I have had, and each one has done the same, that is to say, 34,500 miles in the fifteen months. I am so pleased with your cars that I am taking delivery of my fifth Ford on 1st May." (Letter No. 1052.)

Ford owners

"This is my fifth Ford car, and it gives me the greatest pleasure to add that the consideration which your Company gives to each customer is worthy of the highest praise." (Letter No. 1056.)

will tell you

"As a garage mechanic might I squeeze in a word of congratulation ? I have all kinds of cars pass through my hands, but the one car that stands for efficiency and simplicity is the Ford. In my estimation it is the finest investment any individual might make." (Letter No. 1042.)

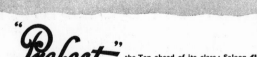

THE *"Prefect"* the Ten ahead of its class : Saloon **£145**, Double-Entrance Saloon **£152 10s.**, Touring Car **£155**; prices at works. The only British Ten under **£150**.

FORD MOTOR COMPANY LIMITED, DAGENHAM, ESSEX. LONDON SHOWROOMS: 88 REGENT ST., W.I

Features of the Ford Prefect

A Staff artist of " The Light Car" contributes this " Illustrated Specification" which discloses in a simple and direct fashion the leading—

LEADING FEATURES

(1) RESERVAC: Vacuum tank for windscreen wipers. (2) ENGINE: 4-cyl., 63·5 mm. x 92·5 mm. (1,172 c.c.). Develops 30·1 b.h.p. at 4,000 r.p.m. Chain-driven camshaft, side valves, 3-bearing crankshaft and non-adjustable tappets. Thermo-siphon, fan-assisted cooling. Entire unit mounted on rubber at 4 points. (3) CARBURETTER: Downdraught, incorporating easy-starting device. (4) CLUTCH: Single dry-plate. (5) GEARBOX: Selective sliding, with synchromesh on intermediate gears. Ratios, 5·5, 9·71 and 16·89 to 1; reverse, 22·08 to 1. (6) BATTERY: 6-volt, 63 amp.-hr. (7) BODY: All-steel welded. Cellulose finish, safety-glass screen cloth-lined roof and cloth upholstery. (8) REAR AXLE: ¾-floating, spiral-bevel. (9) PETROL TANK: 7-gallon capacity. (10) TYRES: 5·00 x 16, low-pressure. (11) SUSPENSION: Transverse leaf springs. (12) BRAKES: Mechanical with 10-in. drums; handbrake operates on rear wheels only. (13) SHOCK-ABSORBERS: Double-acting hydraulic. (14) RADIUS RODS. (15) TORQUE TUBE: Enclosed drive. (16) PROPELLER SHAFT: Centre bearing.

The tiny English Ford 4-cylinder car is shown here in a cutaway view. These cars are manufactured by the Ford factory in England. A very few have ever entered the United States. — Clymer.

"I have tried many oils—but it was MOBILOIL that cured Oil-Drag"

He's proved that it pays to insist on Mobiloil and save hard cash! For Oil-Drag is not merely a thief of power, he is a thief of petrol and oil. The certain way to cure Oil-Drag is to use Mobiloil—the one oil refined by the Clearosol process which purges it of the impurities that *cause* Oil-Drag. Change to Mobiloil today and your car will perform at its peak—full power, lower consumption, and freedom from repair bills.

DRAIN, FLUSH AND REFILL WITH
MOBILOIL —It defeats OIL-DRAG

VACUUM OIL COMPANY LIMITED, LONDON, S.W.1

FINEST CAR VALUE AT £159
(8 H.P.)

1939

LOWEST-PRICED BRITISH COUPÉ

THE NEW *Flying Standard*

A wonderful new Flying Standard—a very worthy addition to the "Eight" range of models! Its exceptional qualities and unique features make this coupé one of the finest examples of value among motor cars today. Features include :—independent front wheel suspension; 60 m.p.h.; 45-48 m.p.g.; roomy two-door four-seater body; folding head, easily operated; wind-up door windows; ample luggage space; Triplex Glass all round; Dunlop Tyres; tax £6.

Other 8 h.p. models: Saloon £129, Saloon de Luxe £139,
Open Tourer £125. (All prices ex works.)

THE STANDARD MOTOR COMPANY LTD., COVENTRY

West End Showrooms:
"Standard Cars", 37 Davies St., Grosvenor Sq., W.1. Tel. Mayfair 5011

SETS NEW SPEED RECORD   1939

New speed records for racing cars of three liters displacement were established on the Reichsautobahn between Dessau and Bitterfield, Germany, by Rudolf Caracciola in this Mercedes-Benz car. He made the flying kilometer at an average speed (for both directions) of 247.46 m.p.h. and the flying mile at the average speed of 248.286 m.p.h.

" I'm in the deuce of a dilemma, Bertie; if I keep this exhaust system I can't hear my radio and if I keep the radio bang goes one of the finest crackles on the roads."

MIDGET
DROPHEAD
COUPÉ

MG

SAFETY FAST!

ADMIRALTY ARCH, LONDON

1939

"Had an argument the other day with a journalist friend of mine who had stated that the gap between the high performance car and the normal car is closing.

I wonder if it really is! In price it may be so. But take an ordinary touring car and compare it with the M.G. for a high speed cross-country run, for those instant accelerations that spell safety, for stability on grease and that general easeful handling that breed brings out in a car. That is where, in my opinion, the M.G. scores."

Cecil Kimber

MANAGING DIRECTOR OF M.G. CARS

M.G. Midget from £222 • 1½-Litre from £280 • 2-Litre from £389 • 2.6-Litre from £442 • (Ex works.) Dunlop, Triplex, Jackall
THE M.G. CAR COMPANY LIMITED • ABINGDON-ON-THAMES, BERKSHIRE • SOLE EXPORTERS — M.I.E. LIMITED • COWLEY • OXFORD • ENGLAND
D 2